Fast
Forward
Writing

LEVEL **3** to LEVEL **4**

Second Edition

Acknowledgements

Acknowledgements for copyright text, artwork, photographs and images on page 120.

Orders: please contact Bookpoint Ltd, 130 Milton Park, Abingdon, Oxon OX14 4SB. Telephone: (44) 01235 827720. Fax: (44) 01235 400454. Lines are open from 9.00am – 6.00pm, Monday to Saturday, with a 24 hour message answering service. You can also order through our website www.hoddereducation.co.uk.

British Library Cataloguing in Publication Data
A catalogue record for this title is available from the British Library

ISBN 0: 0 340 81588 4
ISBN-13: 978 0 340 81588 5

First edition published 2003
This edition first published 2004
Impression number   10 9 8 7 6 5 4 3
Year   2008 2007 2006

Copyright © 2003, 2004 Sue Hackman

Cover artwork by Neil Leslie, Début Art.
Typeset by Endangered Species, Essex.
Printed in Italy for Hodder Murray, a division of Hodder Education, 338 Euston Road, London NW1 3BH.

Sue Hackman

Fast Forward Writing

LEVEL **3** to LEVEL **4**

Second Edition

Hodder Murray

A MEMBER OF THE HODDER HEADLINE GROUP

Assessment Packs and other Fast Forward *books*

Please note that Assessment Packs are available providing short 'before and after' tests for puplis aiming to move from one level to the next. These tests provide teachers with useful pupil profiles and provide pupils with clear targets. Assessment tasks are built into each masterclass of the **Fast Forward Writing** series.

Fast Forward Level 3 to Level 4	**ISBN 0 340 81585 X**
Fast Forward Level 3 to Level 4 Assessment Pack	**ISBN 0 340 78025 8**
Fast Forward Level 4 to Level 5	**ISBN 0 340 81586 8**
Fast Forward Level 4 to Level 5 Assessment Pack	**ISBN 0 340 80363 0**
Fast Forward Level 5 to Level 6	**ISBN 0 340 81587 6**
Fast Forward Level 5 to Level 6 Assessment Pack	**ISBN 0 340 80366 5**
Fast Forward Writing Level 3 to Level 4	**ISBN 0 340 81588 4**
Fast Forward Writing Level 4 to Level 5	**ISBN 0 340 81192 7**

Contents

A. Shaping sentences   **1**

1. Starting sentences   **1**

- Starting with *where*, *when* or *how*   1
- Starting with ING or ED   4
- Starting with LY   5

2. Sequencing sentences   **7**

- Sequencing a sentence   7
- Building a longer sequence   10

3. Add-ons, drop-ins and asides   **13**

- Add-ons   13
- Drop-ins   15
- Asides   16

4. Building sentences   **19**

- Action sentences   19
- Russian doll sentences   21
- Commas   22

5. Ending sentences   **25**

- Ending with a fact   25
- Ending with an action   26
- Ending with a reiteration   27
- Ending with a detail   28
- Ending with a surprise   29

B. Grabbing the reader   **31**

6. Appealing to the senses   **31**

- Using touch, sight, sound, smell and taste   31
- Recreating sensations   33

7. Appealing to feelings   **37**

- Words that make judgements   37
- Playing on emotions   38
- Influencing feelings   40

8. Steering the reader   **43**

- Using signs to steer the reader   43
- Using layout to steer the reader   43
- Using words to steer the reader   46

C. Putting on the style   49

9. The confident voice   **49**

- Using assertions   50
- Using commands   51
- Using confident expressions   52

10. The formal voice   **55**

- Using passive verbs   56
- Using precise vocabulary   57
- Keeping an even tone   58
- Formal writing   59

11. Plain clear writing   **61**

- Diagnosing the problem   63
- Simplifying your writing   64
- How to write clearly   65

D. Telling   67

12. Ways of telling   **67**

- Different ways of telling   67
- Using time   68
- Using reflection   70

13. Telling by showing   **73**

- Looking from the outside in   75
- Using symbols   77

14. Definition   **79**

- Defining character   79
- Defining places   82
- Defining statements   83

E. Writing on demand   85

15. Planning writing in the test   85

- Getting a fix on the question   85
- Making a quick plan   86
- Timing the writing   88
- Preparing starters   89

16. Composing paragraphs   91

- In order of event   92
- Making a point   92
- Categorising information   93
- By order of importance   93

17. Checking   97

- Knowing your own weak spots   97
- Keeping an eye on errors   98
- A checking routine   98
- Making neat corrections   99

F. Notes   100

18. Notes to the pupil   100

19. Notes to parents and helpers   110

20. Notes to the teacher   116

A. Shaping sentences

Aims of this unit of work

- To enhance pupils' ability to manipulate sentence structure to extend and enhance meaning
- To develop pupils' ability to use sentence sequence, subordination and endings for effect
- To improve the variety and imagination of expression

Objectives addressed (by year)

Year 6 objectives

S1.2	Order
S1.3	Construction of complex sentences
S1.5	Complex sentences
S1.6	Sophisticated punctuation
S2.2	Structure of paragraphs
S2.8	Evoking responses
S2.3	Revise complex sentences
S3.1	Management of complex sentences
S3.4	Control of complex sentences

Year 7 objectives

S1	Subordinate clauses
S3	Boundary punctuation
S8	Starting paragraphs
S9	Main point of a paragraph
S10	Paragraph structure
S11	Sentence variety
S12	Sequencing paragraphs
Wr14	Evocative description

Year 8 objectives

S1	Complex sentences
S2	Variety of sentence structure
S6	Grouping sentences
Wr2	Anticipate reader reaction

Delivery

The unit is organised in five masterclasses of around 2 hours each for use by individuals or small groups working co-operatively:

Masterclass 1: Starting sentences
Masterclass 2: Sequencing sentences
Masterclass 3: Add-ons, drop-ins and asides
Masterclass 4: Building sentences
Masterclass 5: Ending sentences

Total: 10 hours

Enhance this unit by introducing sentences from texts known to the class, or by composing examples together on the board.

B. *Grabbing the reader*

Aims of this unit of work

- To help writers to appeal to the reader's senses
- To help writers to engage the reader's emotions
- To create considerate writers who guide their readers through the text

Objectives addressed (by year)

Year 6 objectives

T1.3	Personal responses
T2.1	Narrative structure
T2.8	Evoking responses
T2.18	Construct arguments

Year 7 objectives

Wd20	Connectives
R6	Active reading
Wr7	Narrative devices
Wr8	Infer and deduce
Wr10	Organise texts appropriately
Wr14	Evocative description

Year 8 objectives

S7	Cohesion and coherence
Wr6	Figurative language
Wr7	Establish the tone
Wr10	Effective information
Wr13	Present a case persuasively

Delivery

The unit is organised in three masterclasses of around 2 hours each for use by individuals or small groups working co-operatively:

Masterclass 6: Appealing to the senses
Masterclass 7: Appealing to feelings
Masterclass 8: Steering the reader

Total: 6 hours

Enhance this unit by studying texts known to the class, or by composing examples together on the board.

- In Masterclass 6, collections of simple but visually interesting objects such as marbles or pebbles would be helpful as a stimulus.
- In Masterclass 7, a display of promotional leaflets would be useful.
- In Masterclass 8, a telephone directory would be a useful reference to show original layouts in their context.

C. Putting on the style

Aims of this unit of work

- To develop a confident voice in writing
- To develop a formal voice in writing
- To achieve a plain clear style of writing

Objectives addressed (by year)

Year 6 objectives

S1.3	Passive verbs
S2.1	Passive verbs
S2.2	Formal language choice
S3.3	Revise formal style
T2.20	Standard English
T3.20	Impersonal writing
T3.22	Appropriate style and form

Year 7 objectives

Wd14	Word meaning in context
Wd21	Subject vocabulary
S5	Active or passive voice
S17	Standard English
Wr1	Drafting process

Year 8 objectives

Wd7c	Words in context
Wd9	Specialist vocabulary
Wd12	Formality and word choice
S10	Adapting text types
S12	Degrees of formality
Wr12	Formal description

Delivery

The unit is organised in three masterclasses of around 2 hours each for use by individuals or small groups working co-operatively:

Masterclass 9: The confident voice
Masterclass 10: The formal voice
Masterclass 11: Plain clear writing

Total: 6 hours

Enhance this unit by studying texts known to the class, or by composing examples together on the board.

D. *Telling*

Aims of this unit of work

- To expand the repertoire of narrative approaches
- To improve the use of description and reflection
- To bring greater definition to writing

Objectives addressed (by year)

Year 6 objectives

T1.2	Viewpoint
T1.6	Manipulate perspective
T2.1	Narrative structure
T3.1.1	Narrative

Year 7 objectives

R6	Active reading
R8	Infer and deduce
R12	Character, setting and mood
R14	Language choices
Wr6	Characterisation
Wr7	Narrative devices
Wr11	Present information
Wr14	Evocative description

Year 8 objectives

R7	Implied and explicit meaning
Wr5	Narrative commentary
Wr6	Figurative language

Delivery

The unit is organised in three masterclasses of around 2 hours each for use by individuals or small groups working co-operatively:

Masterclass 12: Ways of telling
Masterclass 13: Telling by showing
Masterclass 14: Definition

Total: 6 hours

Enhance this unit by studying extracts from stories and novels known to the class, or by composing examples together on the board.

E. *Writing on demand*

Aims of this unit of work

- To prepare for the demands of tests and work in timed conditions
- To promote effective planning and preparation
- To support extended writing

Objectives addressed (by year)

Year 6 objectives

T2.2	Paragraph structure ideas
T3.21	Linking paragraphs

Year 7 objectives

Wd8	Personal spelling
S8	Starting paragraphs
S9	Main point of paragraph
S10	Paragraph structure
S12	Sequencing paragraphs
Wr2	Planning formats
Wr10	Present information
Wr12	Develop logic

Year 8 objectives

R10	Development of key ideas
S6	Grouping sentences
S7	Cohesion and coherence
Wr1	Effective planning
Wr10	Effective information

For **Year 9** pupils preparing for KS3 tests, the unit directly addresses objectives:

9S5	Shape paragraphs rapidly
9S6	Paragraph organisation
9Wr1	Review own writing
9Wr3	Formal essay

Delivery

The unit is organised in three masterclasses, of which the first two last 2 hours and the other around 1 hour. The work is probably best undertaken as a series of discussion tasks, but pupils should undertake the more substantial activities independently so that the teacher can establish how well prepared they are for test conditions.

Masterclass 15: Planning writing in the test
Masterclass 16: Composing paragraphs
Masterclass 17: Checking

Total: 5 hours

SHAPING SENTENCES

1. Starting sentences

In this masterclass you will learn how to:

- start your sentences in different ways
- make your sentences more interesting and varied
- help your reader to tune in.

1. Starting with *where*, *when* or *how*

Here is an idea for making your sentences more varied and interesting. Instead of starting with a person or thing, start by saying *where*, *when* or *how* it happened.

Examples of *where* starts

> Over in the other corner, Mike was...
>
> Back at the club, the men were listening to...
>
> Somewhere in the distance, they could hear...

Examples of *how* starts

> Slowly, he raised his hands...
>
> Without a moment's hesitation, he leapt up and...
>
> Taking care to empty all the pockets, he put the jacket into...

Examples of *when* starts

> Later that evening, they began to...
>
> Next, you must...
>
> After completing step 2, move on to...

Readers find this information helpful in getting an idea of what is about to happen.

Help ≫

Commas
- Notice the way these sentence starts are followed by a comma.
- The comma is used to mark the start of the main sentence.

Example

There are eleven sentences in this extract. How many of them start with the main subject (usually a person or a thing) and how many start by saying *where*, *when* or *how*?

Burying a dog

He pulled a shovel out of the wagon bed and walked back to the rocks at the foot of the mountainside. He selected a rock about the size of a wash basin and, straining, rolled it on its side. Then, kneeling, he began to dig with his one good arm. In a few minutes, he was exhausted but he kept it up.

The dog was wrapped in Swanson's saddle blanket when he laid him in the hole. He half wished the old nun was awake so she could say some words over it. He didn't know what to say. He sat for a long time staring at the mound under the blanket. Finally, he said, 'I'll miss you, dog.'

When the hole was filled up, he rolled the heavy stone back into place, and brushed the sand around it so it wasn't possible to know the rock had ever been moved. Then he went closer to the edge of the mountain and sat thinking for a while.

From *St Agnes Stand* by **Thomas Eidson**

About half begin with the subject and half begin with the *where*, *when* or *how*.

Look more closely at the sentences that start with *where*, *when* or *how* and find the one that includes both *when* and *how*. All the others start with *when*.

Help ▶▶

A good rule of thumb: about half your sentences should start with *where*, *when* or *how*.

Try it

Write a paragraph or two describing someone struggling to stop a big leak from a tap. About half your sentences should start with *when*, *how* or *where*. Aim for six to ten sentences.

Start:

Jay turned the tap. A moment later, he found himself standing beneath...

Share your writing and discuss what works best.

Hot Tip ≫

Make a list of possible sentence starters to use, such as:

• For a few seconds...
• Within moments...
• Under the sink...
• Without thinking...

2. Starting with ING or ED

Here's another way to start sentences: start with a verb that ends in ING or ED. Or to put it another way, tell your reader something about the state of your character or subject.

Examples of ING starts

> **Thinking of the time, Julia excused herself and...**
> **Taking the next turn left, walk along Park Road and...**
> **Shivering, Leila pulled her coat around her...**

INGs are good for giving instructions and directions as well as for telling you why people do what they do.

Examples of ED starts

> **Overjoyed with his success, Dom called...**
> **Defeated, the Celts withdrew to...**
> **Refreshed, we set out once more...**

EDs are good for telling you the state things are in, for example overjoyed, defeated, refreshed.

Help ▶▶

Commas again

Notice the way these sentence starters are followed by a comma.

The comma is used to mark the start of the main sentence.

Try it

Try improving this extract by changing any two of the sentences into ING or ED starts.

> **The thief was surprised by the alarm and took to his heels. He headed down the street and turned into a nearby alley. He ran with desperate speed and vaulted the wall at the end.**

Next, add three more sentences up to the point where the thief stops because he is out of breath. Make at least one of these extra sentences an ING or ED start.

Read aloud the original and your new version. Which sounds better?

3. Starting with LY

Here's another way to start a sentence. Use an adverb ending in LY. Adverbs tell the reader how something is done.

Examples of LY starts

Quickly mix the chocolate with the sauce.

Defiantly, the Goths launched an attack on the main gate.

Slowly, the fox emerged from its lair.

Inevitably, the truth came out.

Commas yet again

Notice that commas mark the start of the main sentence.

Commands are an exception because the verb comes first. When the adverb is next to its verb, it doesn't need a comma.

Try it

Rephrase these instructions so that at least two of the sentences start with an LY.

Open the package with great care and remove the box from the wrapping.

Place it on a flat surface, red side upwards.

Pull the release catch with firm, even pressure.

Test it

Write seven sentences reporting the most exciting moment of a wrestling match, duel or other one-on-one contest.

Four of the sentences should start with *when*, *where*, *how*, *ING*, *ED*, or *LY*.

Hot Tip

Reading back

Keep reading back your work so far to check that it reads well. Listen for what will sound good at the start of the next sentence. The trick is not to let it get repetitive. Mix the different kinds of starts.

What you get marks for

Four sentences start with *where*, *when*, *how*, *ING*, *ED* or *LY*	4 marks
The start words make sense and add something	4 marks
The starts are varied and don't sound repetitive	2 marks
Total	**10 marks**

2. Sequencing sentences

In this masterclass you will learn how to:

- sequence a sentence so it adds to the meaning
- pack a punch at the end of a sentence
- build up powerful paragraphs.

1. Sequencing a sentence

Look at the order in which the information is given in this sentence:

Journey

It took three hours, and several words of guidance, before he came to the little blue lake.

From *The Amber Spyglass* **by Philip Pullman**

The little blue lake comes right at the end of the sentence, just as it came right at the end of the journey. It recreates the experience of the journey by making the reader wait for the main moment.

Look closer

Explain how the sequence of these two sentences reflects their meaning:

Storm

And now the sky was laced with lightning, and then the first almighty crack of thunder hit their eardrums like an axe.

From *The Amber Spyglass* by Philip Pullman

Climbing a mountain

The little road shrinks to a path, the path to a track and as the last visible farm house shrinks far behind, the sense of space is tremendous and is forever.

From *Journey through Britain* by John Hillaby

How does each of the sentences pack a punch at the end? Look for examples of:

- powerful vocabulary
- sound effects
- repetition
- simile and metaphor.

Try it

1 Work in pairs to put these two ideas for sentences in good order:

● A sentence that describes someone slipping into drowsiness and then into sleep.

● A sentence in which someone looks inside a box and gets a nasty surprise. Pack the surprise into the end, without relying on an exclamation mark.

2 Improve your two sentences using any of the advice in the Help boxes below.

3 Share and compare your work with two other groups. Agree what made the most successful sentences.

Help ▶▶

Packing a punch

- Keep the reader guessing.
- Leave the surprise till last.
- Use powerful words at the end.
- Use vivid words, e.g. *colours.*
- Use sound effects to catch the ear.
- Be brief to add shock value.
- Keep it plain in the serious moments.
- Play on the readers' feelings by helping them to share the surprise or emotion, e.g. a *significant detail*, a *big idea*.

Help ▶▶

Avoid cop-outs

Some DON'Ts:

- Don't rely on an exclamation mark to provide the punch.
- Don't go over the top with childish scares, e.g. *a huge black insect with drooling jaws and claws covered in blood.*
- Don't rely on empty exaggerations, e.g. *really, very, incredibly.*
- Don't tell the reader how to feel, e.g. *It was so shocking!*
- Don't use boring clichés, e.g. *He got the fright of his life; he nearly jumped out of his socks; his hair stood on end.*

2. Building a longer sequence

You have learnt how sentences can be ordered to help meaning. You can order paragraphs in the same way.

Try breaking your ideas into key moments, like a cartoonist might break a story into boxes. It is easy to write events in the order they happen; the trick is in deciding how to show them.

Use the cartoon below to build the opening paragraph of a novel in which someone is woken from a deep sleep by knocking at the door.

1. Lost in sleep, dreaming
2. Unsettled by knocking in the dream
3. Tries to ignore it
4. Forcing herself to come round
5. Realising what's happening
6. Getting up to answer

1 Write six well-sequenced sentences, one for each stage of the waking up.

2 Read them to see if they work well together. Adjust them so that they do.

3 Check for cop-outs.

4 See if you can use any other techniques for packing punches.

Try it

Write a paragraph about arriving for your first day at school.
Remember how big and noisy it seemed and how nervous you felt.

1   Think what you are going to say in five steps, which will be your sentences, and make a note of them so you don't forget.

2   Draft each sentence so that the sequence helps the meaning, and packs punches in the right places.

3   Check that the sentences work well together.

4   Check for cop-outs.

5   Write up in neat.

Hot Tip ▶▶

Writing inside the head

The best writers rehearse special sentences in their head before they write.

- Try saying your sentence in your head first.
- Try shifting it around in your head to find the best way of saying it.

Doing this means fewer corrections on the page.

It also means you are more likely to get full stops in the right place.

Test it

Write a paragraph that describes a cyclist just reaching the top of the hill, then picking up speed as he travels downhill.

Start: *The cyclist heaved the last few metres to the top of the hill and...*

Hot Tip

- Spend a minute or so planning the steps like cartoon frames.
- Move directly in to the action; you don't have to set the scene.
- Save some time at the end for reading it back. Listen for false notes and put them right.

What you get marks for

Sentences sequenced to reflect meaning	2 marks
Well-packed punches	2 marks
Sentences follow each other well	2 marks
No cop-outs	1 marks
It's not over the top	1 marks
The overall effect is convincing	2 marks
Total	**10 marks**

3. Add-ons, drop-ins and asides

In this masterclass you will learn how to:

- make your sentences richer by adding detail
- make your sentences more sophisticated by extending ideas in them
- add detail without piling on the adjectives.

1. Add-ons

Make your sentences richer by adding telling detail to the end. Film makers do the same thing by zooming in or using a close-up.

Example

Look at these three sentences. Together, they make the opening paragraph of a novel. In each case, the main clause of the sentence has been underlined. But look at the detail that follows.

On the veranda overlooking the garden, the drive and the gate, <u>they sit together on the creaking sofa–swing</u>, suspended from its iron frame, dangling their legs so that the slippers on their feet hang loose.

Before them, <u>a low round table is covered with a faded cloth</u>, embroidered in the centre with flowers.

<u>The parents sit</u>, rhythmically swinging, back and forth.

From *Fasting, Feasting* by Anita Desai

Slippers suggest home, family and informality. You guess they are at home and married. Can you see other details and what they suggest?

What does detail do?

- It gives a strong, sharp image of the scene.
- It drops hints about place, character and social context.

Try it

Here is another sentence from the same novel:

> <u>Uma flounces off</u>, her grey hair frazzled, her myopic eyes glaring behind her spectacles, muttering under her breath.

The main clause has been underlined. Notice how detail has been added in three extra clauses.

Add detail to these sentence starters using three extra clauses:

The creature roars in anger, its...
Doran lunges at the creature's throat, his...

2. Drop-ins

You can make your writing richer by dropping in telling details and comments.

Here's a sentence describing a woman making a sleeping potion:

She crumbled some dried leaves into it and added three drops of a pale yellow oil.

There's nothing wrong with this sentence. It's a good sentence. But Philip Pullman, in his novel *The Amber Spyglass*, dropped in some extra details that made it better:

Crouching down, she crumbled some dried leaves into it, **two pinches from this bag, one from that,** and added three drops of a pale yellow oil.

From *The Amber Spyglass* **by Philip Pullman**

We knew *what* she was doing, but the drop-in details give us a sharp picture because they tell us *how* she did it.

- We are told that she **crouched**, so we get a picture of her squatting down.
- We are told how she took **two pinches from this bag, one from that,** so we see her move her hands and how much she took.
- We are given enough information to create an image, even a moving image.

It works like a film, following the movements.

Try it

Drop two details into this sentence at the arrows to make the food seem rich and disgusting:

The pig's heart ^ was served ^ with slug gravy.

Drop two details into this sentence to make it sound sinister:

She swivelled round to see what had made the sudden noise.

3. Asides

An 'aside' is when the storyteller breaks off and makes a whispered comment direct to the reader. Spot the 'aside' in this sentence:

> The black fox had watched a moment more – she was not an impetuous hunter – and then, suddenly, without a sound, she had leaped to the nest.

From *The Midnight Fox* by Betsy Byars

The 'aside' in this sentence is *she was not an impetuous hunter*. It is sectioned off very clearly by the dashes and is a complete sentence within a sentence.

An 'aside' is when the narrator takes time out of the story to make a comment directly to you, the reader. Here, the storyteller is giving the reader the benefit of her knowledge.

Try it

Pop an 'aside' into these sentences:

I don't know how long I sat there ^ but it was a long time.

One time my mum and dad had me sit down and make a list of all the things I was afraid of, because they thought that if I wrote all these fears down on paper ^ I would see how foolish my fears were.

See the writer's originals on page 18.

Compare what you added with what the writer added. The author explains things to the reader. Is this what you did?

Using dashes

Use dashes only if you are deliberately cutting away from your sentence to say something as an aside. If you were speaking, this is where you would lower your voice and change your tone. You would hear the change. In writing, you use dashes.

Dashes are dramatic. Don't overuse them.

Look closer

They arrived at Amy's house, and he waited while she changed into jeans. Amy's mother, a tall, thin woman, acknowledged her introduction to Adam without really looking at him – she was on the telephone making arrangements for a committee of some sort – and then she dashed out of the house on the way to another committee meeting. Adam wondered whether he should call his mother. He had told her he'd be late today, detained at a meeting of the Literary Club, but he was a terrible liar.

From *I am the Cheese* by Robert Cormier

- Find an example of an add-on, a drop-in and an aside.
- Strip the sentences in this extract back to basics, so they still make sense, but all the extras have been removed. It can be tricky to decide what is 'in' and what is 'out', so start by removing the obvious extras, then decide which of the other cuts are important to the sense and which are not. Cut out the less important ones.
- Look at the parts you have removed. What do they add? What job do they do?
- Take the stripped-back sentences and fill them out again with different 'extras' of your own. Compare results.
- How do added details influence the meaning of the basic sentence?

▶▶ Test it

Add five sentences to the end of this paragraph in which Adam's father is attacked by a dog. Show what happens next.

Adam took one more step – and the dog attacked, the growl reaching a siren's howl as the animal leaped towards his father. His father stepped aside, one arm outstretched, the dog's teeth ripping the sleeve of his father's jacket. The teeth caught on the jacket for a moment, long enough for his father to fling the animal away, changing its course for an instant. In that instant, his father cried for Adam to run, but...

From *I am the Cheese* by Robert Cormier

What you get marks for

At least three sentences use add-ons, drop-ins or asides	3 marks
The add-ons, drop-ins or asides add sharp, useful detail	3 marks
There are commas or dashes between the main clause and the 'extras'	3 marks
When you read it aloud, it has a pace to match the action	1 mark
Total	**10 marks**

ANSWERS

I don't know how long I sat there – I usually forgot about my watch when I was in the woods – but it was a long time.

From *The Midnight Fox* by Betsy Byars

One time my mum and dad had me sit down and make a list of all the things I was afraid of, because they thought that if I wrote all these fears down on paper – things like being afraid of high places and being afraid of dogs – I would see how foolish my fears were.

From *The Midnight Fox* by Betsy Byars

Hot Tip ▶▶

Writing action

- Action is exciting to watch but boring to read, so give visual details that help the reader to see it in the mind's eye.

- Most writers speed up for action, by using short sentences and by chopping up long sentences into short, breathless sections. Add-ons and drop-ins help with this.

- However, this is not an excuse for using lots of commas incorrectly. You still have to put full stops at the end of sentences.

4. Building sentences

In this masterclass you will learn how to:

- build up a sentence
- match your sentence shape to its content
- punctuate it properly.

1. Action sentences

Action sentences are built around verbs – the 'doing' words. The trick of writing a good action sentence is to choose three or four good verbs that fit together well. Try watching the scene in your mind's eye and choose the verbs for each small step.

For example:

For the start of a race: **poised – tensed – sprang – released.**

Example

For the final blow in a sword fight:
lunged – swung – sliced – thrust.

Then he lunged forward and swung his right arm down, slicing the air before him, thrusting the blade into his opponent's chest.

How to build a verb-based sentence

1 Choose some good verbs.
2 Have the action in your mind.
3 Sequence the verbs.
4 Frame a sentence.
5 Adapt the verbs to suit the tense and position in the sentence.

What might be the key verbs in the following sentence?

A baby fox practises hunting

I have never seen a fiercer fight in my life than the one that baby fox gave that dead bird. He _____1_____ it, _____2_____ it, _____3_____ it this way and that, all the while _____4_____ and _____5_____ to see if anyone or anything was after his prize.

From *The Midnight Fox* by Betsy Byars

Compare your suggestions with the originals on page 24.

Try it

Choose three or four verbs for each of these action sentences:

- For undressing at the end of a long, hot, miserable walk.
- For sinking into a hot bath.
- For relaxing in the bath.

Try using the best of your verbs in three sentences that work together as a paragraph. Use the sentence starters below if they help:

Wearily, he dragged his shirt over his head,...

He let himself sink in the bath, and...

Within moments, he relaxed into...

2. Russian doll sentences

Sometimes writers want to go deeper. They want to take the reader closer, to add detail or explain things to make the reader think hard. To do this, they can build up a sentence in layers, each new clause adding a new angle on the one before. This can be done over several sentences, but fitting it snugly into one sentence allows a writer to unpack all the different points he or she wants to make about a single moment.

Unlike simple add-ons, these sentences don't just add information, they take you deeper into it. They 'unpack' the first idea. Think of this kind of sentence as a Russian doll.

An example:

> **In the end Clara packs her case, loading only one change of clothes but all of her books, and without a goodbye or a backward glance, she leaves by the front door and starts a new life.**

Each new clause reveals something new about her reasons for leaving and her state of mind. It starts simply with a woman packing, but by the end of the sentence we know that she is changing her whole life.

Here are two more sentences. Discuss what is revealed in each layer.

Clara finds herself on a park bench, tired and chilly, suddenly aware that she is entirely on her own now, and in charge of her own life.

Shaking off the first flakes of snow, she forces herself off the bench and strides with a confidence she doesn't feel towards the exit and a sign that says Rooms To Let.

Try it

Build up this opening clause with three more layers that explain how Clara feels when she is forced to give up her new life because she has run out of money:

Clara gazes at the empty purse, then...

Repeat this exercise to describe the moment when Clara realises that in time she will try again, but be better prepared:

Unpacking her clothes, Clara realises...

3. Commas

Commas are often needed to build sentences.

Too often, people use commas when they should use a full stop.

The rule about commas is:

- Use them between items in a list (this can be lists of actions as well as things).
- Use them to mark off your main clause if it is interrupted by a subordinate clause.

More help with commas

At the centre of every sentence is a **main clause**. The main clause covers the main action and who (or what) did it. It may be dressed up with add-ons and drop-ins, but essentially it's about one thing that happens. Left alone, it would be a short sentence, complete with a noun and a verb. The Americans call it an **independent clause**.

The main clause here is underlined:

> Sometimes at night when the rain is beating against the windows of my room, <u>I think about that summer on the farm</u>.

From *The Midnight Fox* by **Betsy Byars**

You can tell which is the main clause because it makes sense on its own.

The other clause – the **subordinate clause** – can't stand alone. You can usually spot it because it starts with a word like *although*, *despite* or *when*, so you know there is more to come. It only makes sense with the main clause. The Americans have a better name for it – a **dependent clause**.

Find the main clause in each of these sentences:

> When I close my eyes, I am once again by the creek watching the black fox come leaping over the green, green grass.
>
> She is light and free as the wind, exactly as she was the first time I saw her.

From *The Midnight Fox* by **Betsy Byars**

Find the answers on page 24.

►► Test it

Write a paragraph of five sentences describing a banquet set with a rich feast. Use extended sentences to suggest the richness and plenty of the banquet.

Menu

Horse tongue with snails

Grilled octopus with ripe bananas

Fresh adder

Stickleback soup

Add your own dishes.

What you get marks for

Each sentence adds depth through detail	2.5 marks
Three sentences contain subordinate clauses	3 marks
Commas are correct (0.5 mark per sentence)	2.5 marks
Overall effect has a sense of richness and plenty	2 marks
Total	**10 marks**

ANSWERS

Verbs

1 shook
2 pulled
3 dragged

4 growling
5 looking.

Main clauses

- I am once again by the creek watching the black fox.
- She is light and free as the wind.

A. SHAPING SENTENCES

5. Ending sentences

In this masterclass you will learn how to:

- end sentences in different ways
- use endings to shape the meaning
- use endings to create an effect.

The last words in a sentence are important because they are left in the memory as the reader moves on. The last words carry extra weight.

1. Ending with a fact

Newspaper articles and information texts often end sentences with facts. The rest of the sentence leads up to the fact.

Example from a newspaper

> **The mystery car that burst into flames in Hurst High Street last Monday has been identified as a silver-plated 1930s vintage Rolls Royce.**

Example from a text book

> **Before 1971, British money consisted of pounds, shillings and pence.**

Try writing the following sentences, ending each one with a fact:

- A sentence in a newspaper that names a missing person.
- A sentence in a newspaper that names the winner of a record prize in a lottery.
- A sentence in a textbook that describes how pollution is caused.
- A sentence in a magazine that gives details of a new CD.

Ending with a fact leaves the reader with the hard facts ringing in the ears. It also sounds sure and well-informed. It gives a ring of authority.

2. Ending with an action

Ending with an action is unusual and gets extra attention. Try shuffling the parts of the sentence around in your head before writing, and try ending it with the verb.

For example:

> A tractor had made giant ruts in the earth, and the ruts had dried hard, so that his feet kept stumbling in.
>
> **From *I'm the King of the Castle* by Susan Hill**

The sentence stumbles at the end, just as he does.

Compare:

The sun was glaring as he stood in the middle of the field.

with the writer's actual sentence:

> He stood in the very middle of it, now, and the sun came glaring down.
>
> **From *I'm the King of the Castle* by Susan Hill**

Putting the action at the end makes the action more powerful than the person or thing that does it. This is a good technique for describing someone who feels powerless, frightened or out of control. For example:

> **Frightened in a dark wood**
>
> They were whispering. After a moment, Kingshaw moved forward a bit farther, pushing the branches aside carefully with his hands, not knowing what he was going to see. He had a sudden vision of things watching him, from in among the trees, of eyes glinting, and spears poised.
>
> **From *I'm the King of the Castle* by Susan Hill**

Every sentence ends in a verb to show that he feels out of control. Things happen that he can't help. He writes like a victim.

- Write three sentences to describe someone panicking in water. Each sentence must end in an action, to emphasise the fear and powerlessness.
- Write three sentences to describe someone face to face with a dangerous animal. Each sentence must end in an action, to emphasise the terror.

3. Ending with a reiteration

For a really strong ending, you can repeat your last idea in different words.

> They seemed to have been closed in here for hours, for ever.
>
> From *I'm the King of the Castle* by Susan Hill

Notice the way *for ever* repeats and even exaggerates *for hours*. It emphasises the feeling of time going on and on.

> He surprised himself, as he spoke in that way, for he was a reticent, even a severe man.
>
> From *I'm the King of the Castle* by Susan Hill

Notice the way *severe* repeats and exaggerates *reticent*. He has looked inside himself and admitted something important. Here are some more sentences that end with a reiteration. Explain how they work, and what they emphasise.

> He thought, I mustn't let Hooper know what I truly think, never, not about anything.

> He had nothing left that was his own, nothing at all.
>
> From *I'm the King of the Castle* by Susan Hill

Write the following sentences, reiterating the last idea for emphasis:

- A sentence in which you decide never to see someone again.
- A sentence that describes the long road ahead.
- A sentence that describes your excitement as a plane takes off.

4. Ending with a detail

Details give the reader a sudden sharp image of the thing described. Adding a detail to the end of the sentence can be very effective because the reader is left with the detail like an experience, without any further explanation. It captures the moment or sensation. For example:

> He wanted the familiar sounds of bells and desk lids and voices calling in the dining hall, the smell and rows of faces.

From *I'm the King of the Castle* by Susan Hill

Notice how the detail about the smell and the rows of faces is flashed up, like a memory. Another example:

> He walked very slowly through the long grass besides the hedge, sending up sudden clouds of white butterflies every so often.

From *I'm the King of the Castle* by Susan Hill

Notice how the clouds of butterflies form an instant picture in the mind.

Now explain the effect of the details at the end of these two sentences:

> **At the circus**
>
> He held the uneaten ice cream in his left hand, and it dripped away down the side of the seat, and onto the floor, in a sweet, sticky trail.
>
> Kingshaw waited for the turn of the lumbering, gentle elephants, and when they came, almost wept, because of the tasselled caps they were made to wear, and the docile expression in their eyes.

From *I'm the King of the Castle* by Susan Hill

Write the following sentences, finishing each one with an added detail that gives a sharp feel of the experience:

- A sentence in which you describe finding one of your first toys at the back of a cupboard.
- A sentence in which you disturb an ants' nest.

5. Ending with a surprise

For impact, put the most dramatic moment at the end. For example:

> In the covered tunnel leading out of the circus tent, among the pushing crowd of people, Kingshaw was violently sick.

From *I'm the King of the Castle* by Susan Hill

The ending has shock value because it comes last and because the word *violently* gives it force.

Explain the surprise endings in these sentences:

> **A childhood memory**
>
> He had been forced to watch as the insects were removed from their poisoned-fume bottles with tweezers, spread out and then pinned down through their horny bodies on to the card.
>
> **Wrongly accused**
>
> It was ludicrous that he could be accused of leading Hooper away; ludicrous, but entirely possible.

From *I'm the King of the Castle* by Susan Hill

Write the following sentences, ending them with a surprise:

- A sentence in which you open a surprise present.
- A sentence in which you are expected to do something but change your mind at the last minute.

 **Test it**)))

Read the extract and study the way each sentence ends.

> It smelled steamy and damp, like a jungle, and there was another smell, too, sweetish and rotten. There was no air. Kingshaw wanted to climb up the bank again, and go on climbing, up and up one of the elm trees until he could see the open sky. They seemed to have been closed in here for hours, for ever. The water moved sluggishly, between the overgrown banks.
>
> From *I'm the King of the Castle* by **Susan Hill**

1 Explain three ways in which the sentence structure helps the reader to experience what it was like.

2 Write a similar paragraph of three sentences in which you describe the effort of walking through thick, soft mud. End each sentence in a way that recreates the experience.

What you get marks for

In question 1

Spotting how the sentence structure works
(0.5 mark per sentence)   2 marks

Explaining clearly the effect on the reader
(0.5 mark per sentence)   2 marks

In question 2

A mark for each sentence that conveys the sensation
of walking through mud   3 marks

Half a mark for each sentence that ends effectively   1.5 marks

Marks for the overall effectiveness of the writing   1.5 marks

Total   **10 marks**

6. Appealing to the senses

In this masterclass you will learn how to:

- use the senses in your writing
- make your reader share the sensations you describe.

1. Using touch, sight, sound, smell and taste

Writers sometimes want their reader to know how something felt. To do this, they stimulate the senses of touch, smell, sound, taste and sight.

Touch is not just touch. It contains elements of:

- texture
- temperature
- pressure.

What are the elements of **sight**, **sound**, **smell** and **taste**?

Example

Here is an example of a writer appealing to the senses:

Hanging out the washing

She paused, gathering some bundle from a basket at her feet, and then with one motion shook out a peacock-blue sari which she began tacking to the washing line. It puffed outwards with a resigned sigh between her hands. She looked as if she was holding up a piece of the sky.

From *Anita and Me* by Meera Syal

The familiar sight of washing is brought to life by the use of:

- colour (*peacock-blue sari*)
- movement (*shook out, puffed outwards*)
- sound (*puffed, sigh*).

Which senses can you find in these extracts?

A childhood memory

The bus coughed to a halt and Roberto made a great show of holding the automatic doors open for the women. They all flew past me in a tornado of perfume and smoke and shiny snappy handbags, pinching my cheek, ruffling my hair, 'Alright chick?… Oooh, she a little doll, isn't she?'

From *Anita and Me* by Meera Syal

Remembering a holiday

Sometimes at night when the rain is beating against the windows of my room, I think about that summer on the farm. It has been five years, but when I close my eyes I am once again by the creek watching the black fox come leaping over the green, green grass. She is as light and free as the wind.

From *The Midnight Fox* by Betsy Byars

Captive

The Orc's clawlike hand gripped Pippin's arms like iron; the nails bit into him. He shut his eyes and slipped back into evil dreams. Suddenly he was thrown to a stony floor again. It was early night, but the slim moon was already falling westward. They were on the edge of a cliff that seemed to look over a sea of pale mist. There was a sound of water falling nearby.

From *The Lord of the Rings (The Two Towers)* by J.R.R. Tolkien

Try It

Remember a particular moment. Choose a moment when there was a lot to see and hear, perhaps a festival, a dinner, a family gathering or a visit to a special place.

Write just three sentences about this moment. Describe what is happening, but conjure up the feel of it by using the senses.

Help ▶▶

Getting started

Stop. Close your eyes. Remember the moment. Relive it.

What can you see, smell, hear, feel or taste?

Think of words and phrases that capture what it was like.

2. Recreating sensations

To recreate a sensation, your use of the senses should be:

- specific – using words that capture the exact quality of the feeling
- evocative – using words that make it feel sharp and real
- interesting – using words that will put things in a new light.

The extract on the following page is about a woman whose hobby is collecting bits of glass washed up on the beach. Here, she looks through her collection. How does the writer appeal to the senses?

Help ▶▶

Look for:
- contrasts between the colour of the pieces
- the exotic names given to the colours
- the sense of touch
- the sense of taste
- the mystery of where they came from.

A collection of sea glass

In the afternoons and early evenings when the tide has drawn off, Honora looks for sea glass. She finds a slim sliver of amethyst and a jewel-like bit of cobalt. She picks up a thick chunk that looks like dirty ice after a long winter, ice that has been skated on and has gone cloudy with use. She fingers a piece the colour of young dandelions and finds shards that look like flower petals: hyacinth and wisteria and lilac. She puts the pieces in her pocket and takes them home and lays them on a windowsill.

She finds a piece that once was a bottle neck. She picks up a delicate shell-like shape with scalloped edges. She touches a shard the color of mint sauce, another that is ice-blue and reminds her of a waterfall frozen in winter. She finds an olive-green that resembles the state of New York, another shard that seems to be made of the salt film that once coated the windows of the house. She discovers whites that are not white at all, but rather blond and eggshell and ivory and pearl. One day she almost misses a piece because it too closely resembles sand. When she picks it up and holds it to the light, she sees that it is a translucent golden colour, seemingly ancient.

She finds scraps of celadon and cucumber and jade, specks of pea and powder and aquamarine. Once she comes upon a chunk that reminds her of dishwater in a sink. She doesn't like the browns, but occasionally she collects a topaz or a tea. Sometimes all there is is brown, and she goes home slightly depressed. She never keeps a piece of sea glass if it hasn't gone cloudy or if it still retains its sharp edges. Those she buries deep in the sand.

If she looks closely at the glass, she can sometimes see the infinitesimal nicks, the imprints of the sand and rocks that have buffeted it. There's a lump with bubbles in it; another piece, blue-violet, in the shape of a bird in flight.

From *Sea Glass* **by Anita Shreve**

Try it

Describe a collection of objects so that the reader can see what is unusual and interesting about them. Use the senses.

Getting going

You can practise this by finding a handful of real objects – pebbles, marbles or shells.

- Close your eyes and **feel** each one in turn. Find two or three words that distinguish its shape and touch from the others.

- Next **look closely** at each one in turn and find two or three words that distinguish its appearance from the others.

- Next consider each one in turn and think **what it reminds you of**, for example the feel of silk, the colour of mustard.

So what do you do if you are in a test and you can't have the real objects? Try this: imagine seeing and touching objects just as if you had real ones there. Invent them in your mind and pretend to touch and feel them one by one.

Test it

Continue the second paragraph and write a third.
You have 20 minutes.

The morning after the party

The party had been in full swing when I went to bed just after midnight. Coming downstairs a little after ten the next morning, I noted that the house was now completely silent, but something felt wrong. Perhaps it was the smell or the silence.

I opened the kitchen door and surveyed the scene...

What you get marks for

For each sense you stimulate (1 mark each)	up to 5 marks
For each unusual, interesting and specific word that captures the feeling (0.5 mark each)	up to 3 marks
For the overall impact on the reader	2 marks
Total	**10 marks**

7. Appealing to feelings

In this masterclass you will learn how to:

- play on your reader's emotions
- influence your reader's reactions
- gain your reader's sympathy.

Writers often want to influence the way readers feel and respond.

A charity leaflet will ask for your pity.

A love letter will ask for your love.

A complaint will try to stir you into action.

A ghost story will try to make you afraid.

But how do they do it?

1. Words that make judgements

Some words have built-in judgements. For example, these words all imply 'wrong':

Can you think of other words that imply:

sin	**evil**
crime	**cruelty**
indefencible	**selfishness**
guilt	**greed**

- goodness, e.g. angelic
- aggression, e.g. brutal.

2. Playing on emotions

Look at the many ways a writer can influence your reactions:

Words that are charged with emotions: *tormented*

Hard-hitting comparisons: *medieval torture*

Words that pass judgement: *It is wrong*

Putting you in the victim's shoes: *we would not dare have done to ourselves*

Expressing strong reactions: *Are supporters of animal experiments really saying*

animal experiments are immoral

pic. © Brian Gunn

Every year in British laboratories, around 3 million animals are tormented and killed in the name of scientific research. They are poisoned, scalded, wounded, blinded, brain damaged and given lethal diseases.
Two thirds will receive no anaesthetic during 'procedures' which are often more suited to a medieval torture chamber than a modern lab.

It is wrong to cause deliberate injury and death to animals, even in the hope of benefiting people. Doing to animals what we would not dare have done to ourselves amounts to cowardice and bullying. Animals feel pain and distress, like we do. Even the Home Office, which regulates the experiments, recognises their suffering.

We hear that animals are *'less intelligent'* than us and so hurting them is *'acceptable'*. It is also argued that humans are the most important species on earth and that this gives us the right. Are supporters of animal experiments really saying that we should be less considerate of those who appear to have a lower intellectual ability? This shameless logic would justify experimenting on mentally deficient human beings.

You would not offer up your own dog or cat for vivisection. Please don't stand by and let other animals suffer.

From a leaflet by Animal Aid, an organisation that campaigns against animal cruelty

Making a direct appeal: *Please don't stand by*

Can you find other examples of the same techniques used in the leaflet?

Try it

Here are some facts about deer hunting. Write a leaflet asking for help to protect deer. Write three or four paragraphs containing at least four of the techniques mentioned opposite.

Red deer hunting

Britain's largest animal

Less than half a million red deer left in Britain

Live for 25 years

In the past, only kings were allowed to hunt red deer

Hunters chase the strongest deer

Hounds break up the herd and separate the chosen deer from the rest

Hunters use mobile phones to keep in touch, and sometimes ride motorbikes

Hound dogs chase the deer

A chase can go 30 miles

The deer is caught when it is too exhausted to go on

Getting going

If you don't know how to start, plan four paragraphs such as:

1 Why the red deer is worth protecting – make the reader feel sympathy.

2 Why the red deer is in danger – make the reader feel anxiety.

3 Why it is wrong to hunt red deer – make the reader feel disgust and anger.

4 How the reader can help – make the reader feel motivated to do something.

Notice how the emotion builds from **sympath**y to **anxiety** to **anger**.

Then write four starters. For example:

• The beautiful red deer is…

• Yet each year, the life of this gentle creature is threatened by…

• Imagine the final minutes of the deer, as…

• You can help by…

3. Influencing feelings

How do you respond to these two pieces of writing?

What tactics are used to influence the reader's feelings?

MONDAYS ARE RED. SADNESS HAS AN EMPTY BLUE SMELL. AND MUSIC CAN TASTE OF ANYTHING FROM BANANA PUREE TO RAT'S PEE. THAT'S WHAT I NEED TO EXPLAIN, STARTING WITH THE DAY IT ALL BEGAN, THE DAY I WOKE UP IN A HOSPITAL BED WITH A KALEIDOSCOPE IN MY HEAD . . .

The back cover of *Mondays are Red* by Nicola Morgan

Help ▶▶

How writers influence your feelings as you read

Writers can:

- choose words that remind you of the feeling
- choose words that make you judge one way or another
- recreate sensations in the way sentences are expressed, e.g. breathless, panicky sentences
- appeal directly to you, and ask you to feel that way
- make you watch the event through one character's eyes so you see it his or her way.

A fight to the death

Qui-Gon blocked one awful stroke and parried another, then struck back. The Sith Lord blocked – and then slammed the wide handle of his lightsaber into Qui-Gon's chin. Qui-Gon staggered backward, half-dazed from the force of the unexpected blow. The Sith Lord grinned in triumph. Reversing his lightsaber, he struck Qui-Gon through.

Qui-Gon crumpled to the floor.

'No!' Obi-Wan screamed. The sound echoed strangely, almost as if some other voice had joined his in crying out the same desperate denial. But the laser wall was down at last, and Obi-Wan had no more time for thinking. He leaped forward to face the Sith Lord.

Alone.

From *The Phantom Menace* by Patricia Wrede

Try it

Advertising challenge

Your job is persuading people to buy unpopular products that no one else has managed to sell. There are three tasks and you must use a range of tactics to persuade people to buy the goods.

1   Make up attractive names for nail varnish colours that no one wants to buy.

2   Write a radio advertisement that will persuade your listener to buy a pack of these nasty nail varnishes.

3   The boss is asking why only 30 box sets were sold. Write a memo to convince him that 30 packs was a good number, and you deserve a pay rise.

Horrible slimy green colour

Nasty snot colour

Sludgy brown colour

Dark orange, with hard crumbs of glitter

Bright yellow, very unpleasant

MEMORANDUM

To: M.Y. Bigboss
From: M.E. Worklittle
Re: Varnish sales success story

Thank you for your call yesterday, and the interest you have shown in…

Once you have finished, check your work against the tactics listed for influencing your reader. How many did you use? Can you see ways of using the others so you don't rely on just one or two?

Test it

Manhunt!

Manhunt! is a new and cruel game for the very rich in which a team of three paying adults hunt down a poor person on the run.

Write three short separate paragraphs:

1 An advertisement for the game (up to six lines).

2 A paragraph to gain the reader's sympathy, in which you describe the experience of the person on the run when he or she realises the hunters are close.

3 A paragraph to gain the reader's approval, in which you describe the experience of a hunter when he or she realises he or she is close.

What you get marks for

Paragraph 1

Use of two or three words that make the game sound fun, thrilling or interesting	1 mark
Use of a direct appeal to reader	1 mark
Use of two other tactics (0.5 mark each)	up to 1 mark

Paragraph 2

Use of two or three words that suggest the fear	1 mark
Use of sentences structured for fast, panicky feel	1 mark
Use of two other tactics (0.5 mark each)	up to 1 mark

Paragraph 3

Use of two or three words that make the game sound thrilling	1 mark
Use of two other tactics (1 mark each)	up to 2 marks
Overall effect is a positive image	1 mark
Total	**10 marks**

B. GRABBING THE READER

8. Steering the reader

In this masterclass you will learn how to:

- use signs to steer your reader through the text
- use layout to show your reader how the text is organised
- use words to guide your reader through the ideas.

Introduction

Every time you write, you need to guide the reader through your ideas. You can do this using:

Signs, e.g. arrows and bullet points.

Layout, e.g. paragraphs and sub-headings.

Words, e.g. first, next.

Useful signs tell readers how the writing is divided up, where the shifts of topic occur and how it all fits together.

1. Using signs to steer the reader

Writers help readers to find their way around the text by using:

- numbering
- labelled diagrams
- arrows
- underline, bold or italics on special words
- bullet points.

2. Using layout to steer the reader

Writers help the reader to see the shape and order by using:

- space between sections
- headings
- columns
- centring and justifying
- lines between sections
- sub-headings
- boxing key points.

Example

How are signs and layout used to steer the reader through this text?

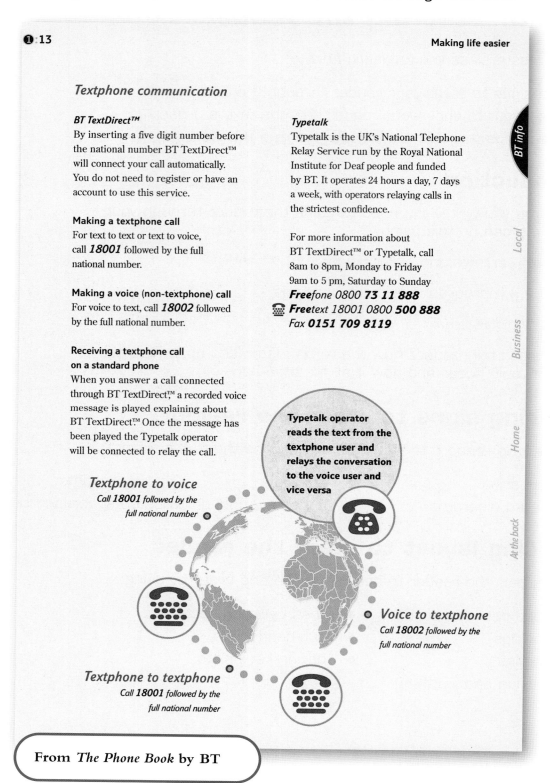

❶:13

Textphone communication

BT TextDirect™
By inserting a five digit number before the national number BT TextDirect™ will connect your call automatically. You do not need to register or have an account to use this service.

Making a textphone call
For text to text or text to voice, call **18001** followed by the full national number.

Making a voice (non-textphone) call
For voice to text, call **18002** followed by the full national number.

Receiving a textphone call on a standard phone
When you answer a call connected through BT TextDirect,™ a recorded voice message is played explaining about BT TextDirect.™ Once the message has been played the Typetalk operator will be connected to relay the call.

Typetalk
Typetalk is the UK's National Telephone Relay Service run by the Royal National Institute for Deaf people and funded by BT. It operates 24 hours a day, 7 days a week, with operators relaying calls in the strictest confidence.

For more information about BT TextDirect™ or Typetalk, call
8am to 8pm, Monday to Friday
9am to 5 pm, Saturday to Sunday
Freefone 0800 **73 11 888**
Freetext 18001 0800 **500 888**
Fax **0151 709 8119**

Textphone to voice
Call **18001** followed by the full national number

Typetalk operator reads the text from the textphone user and relays the conversation to the voice user and vice versa

Voice to textphone
Call **18002** followed by the full national number

Textphone to textphone
Call **18001** followed by the full national number

BT info

Local

Business

Home

At the back

From *The Phone Book* by BT

Try it

Here are the words that explain how to make an emergency call in the BT telephone directory. On a clean sheet, show how you would lay out the page to guide the reader. Alternatively, lay it out on a computer screen.

In an emergency, call 999.

1. Lift the telephone handset and dial 999. You may also use 112 as an alternative to 999. 112 is now used in all European Union countries to contact the emergency services.

2. Tell the BT operator which of the following emergency services you want. fire police ambulance coastguard mountain rescue cave rescue

3. Wait for the BT operator to connect you to the emergency service.

4. Tell the emergency service: where the trouble is; what the trouble is; where you are; and the number of the phone you are using.

Textphone users
To contact the emergency relay service using BT TextDirect™ Freetext 18000.

Never make a false call.

You risk the lives of others who really need help and it's against the law. You can also be traced immediately to the phone where the call came from.

To contact the police, fire brigade or rescue services in a non-emergency situation, or your gas, water or electricity supplier, see the alphabetical listing in section 3.

From *The Phone Book* by BT

Afterwards, compare your page with the version in a telephone directory.

3. Using words to steer the reader

Even without signs and layout, writers can still steer readers with just words:

- starting each paragraph by pointing out what it will be about
- using connectives to link up events.

Example

There is no need to buy expensive green plants. Instead, grow your own by taking a leaf cutting. First, find a healthy plant and gently pull away a leaf with its stem. It should break off at the base. Now leave it for a day so the break dries up. Meanwhile, fill a small plant pot with a mixture of sand and peat. Push the dried leaf stem into the mixture then cover it with gravel. When the leaf starts to grow, replant it in ordinary compost.

- Four of these sentences start with words that guide you through the time sequence. The first one is *First*. Can you find the other three?
- In the last sentence, the time sequence is backed up by two words in the middle of the sentence – can you find them?
- The second sentence follows on from the first but not by order of time. Which word tells you the relationship between the first and second sentence? What is the relationship?

Time guides

Words that act as time guides include:

- Before
- First
- Next
- Then
- Later
- Meanwhile
- Afterwards

There are other guides, too:

Point of view guides

Examples:

- On one hand
- On the other hand
- Alternatively

Cause and effect guides

Examples:

- As a result
- Because of
- Consequently

Try it

Here are notes for making a compost heap.

Write them up into a guide *without* numbers or pictures. Instead, use guide-words to lead the reader through it.

How to start a compost heap
Wooden container, 1 square metre
Big air holes at bottom
Bottom layer – twiggy material
Layer of grass clippings on top of twigs
Manure on top of that
Household waste on top of that
No meat, fat, twigs
Gets warm in two weeks
Stir it around every week
Ready in 3 months

⏵⏵ Test it))

Write a short leaflet for a one-hour walking tour of a working farm. Use the details on the map to write the guide using words only. Say where to go, and how long to spend at each place.

You have 25 minutes.

What you get marks for

Use of time guides (0.5 mark each)	3 marks
Use of paragraphs to separate each stage	2 marks
Use of other separating devices, e.g. lines, arrows	1 mark
Use of print techniques, e.g. bold, special fonts	1 mark
Other layout devices	1 mark
Overall fluency and effect of writing	2 marks
Total	**10 marks**

9. The confident voice

In this masterclass you will learn how to:

- write in a confident voice
- use assertions and commands
- use expressions of confidence.

There are many times when you have to write in a confident voice. For example:

- to give an expert opinion
- to give a clear explanation
- to give a presentation.

For these kinds of writing, you need to sound as though you know what you are talking about. Even if you are nervous in person, you can learn how to express yourself confidently.

Hot Tip ▸▸

Dressing up in a confident voice

- Imagine yourself doing the voice-over for a TV documentary. Adopt that style.

- Imagine a well-known expert giving a lecture to a live audience. Try writing in that style for that person.

- Get a feel for the style by reading aloud a good example. If you have to write a history essay, read a page of a history book. If you have to write a town guide, find a leaflet in the local tourist office. If you have to write a review, read one in the Sunday newspaper first. Soak up the style and then start writing yourself in the same voice.

Channel 4's Time Team

1. Using assertions

An assertion is a statement that is given as an absolute fact. These are all assertions:

Smoking is bad for you.

Smoking is good for you.

People have lived in Surrey for 450,000 years.

People have lived in Surrey since last Friday.

Two of them are completely incorrect, but they are asserted as facts.

Which five of the sentences below are assertions?

Assertion

An assertion often:

- gets to the point quickly
- uses short strong words and sentences
- uses a plain strong verb such as *is, are, was, were, has, have* – this suggests that it is an obvious fact
- sometimes uses value words like *good, bad, wrong, right*
- mentions the subject at or near the start – this makes you sound fearless
- mentions the opinion or fact at or near the end – this makes it sound final.

a Some experts think that bad behaviour is linked to diet.

b Eating spinach makes you strong.

c Carrots are good for the eyesight.

d I drink cocoa because it helps me to sleep at night.

e New Chocsnooze is the right choice for a healthy night's sleep.

f Too many sugars may lead to tooth decay.

g Too many sweets lead to tooth decay.

h You are what you eat.

Find the correct answers on page 54.

Write these sentences as assertive openings:

- The opening sentence of a paragraph that argues for fining the parents or guardians of pupils who truant.
- The opening sentence of a leaflet urging people to recycle their paper.
- The opening sentence of a review of a new CD.

2. Using commands

Instruct the reader what to do. It puts you in control.

An example of a writer telling the reader what to do:

> People have lived in Surrey for about 450,000 years – an almost unimaginable timescale. Picture it as the twelve hours of a clock-face and life since the Industrial Revolution represents just seconds of time.

From *Hidden Depths* by Roger Hunt

The first sentence is an assertion, but the second sentence is an instruction. It asks the reader to imagine something. It sounds confident because the writer assumed he has the right to do it, that he is in authority.

Here is another example. What does it make the reader do in his or her mind?

> Visit any Surrey village or town and there is likely to be a church or some other focus of worship. One may hear the sound of bells drifting on the breeze, a bride and groom may be standing in a shower of confetti, mourners may be brushing away tears or a baby may be howling with the shock of baptism. It is sobering to realise that all these sights and sounds are ephemeral*.
>
> *ephemeral – soon pass, don't last

From *Hidden Depths* by Roger Hunt

Help ▶▶

Commands

Commands generally start with an imperative verb. Here are some familiar examples of sentences starting with an imperative verb:

Stir the eggs and flour together.

Take the next turning left.

Put down your gun.

Lift the bonnet.

Say thank you.

Commands tend to be short, simple and direct, because you want the reader to understand and follow the order.

When you tell the reader what to do, you take control but you also help him or her to join in. You guide the reader's imagination and give him or her something to do.

- Write two or three sentences asking the reader to imagine what he or she would see in the same spot if time slipped back 1,000 years.
- Write two or three sentences asking the reader to think about the consequences of laying tram lines in your nearest town.

3. Using confident expressions

Spot the expressions in this sentence that make the writer sound confident:

Of course, we now know that the Vikings were intelligent and cultured people.

Of course – this makes it sound as if it's obvious and well known.

we – says it's not just a personal opinion – everyone knows!

now know – suggests that the truth is out.

Confident expressions

- of course
- naturally
- certainly
- without doubt
- without question
- definitely
- in truth
- in all honesty
- frankly
- positively

Confident writers also make quick clear judgements:

The Normans were <u>excellent</u> builders but <u>poor</u> rulers.

Words of judgement

- good
- bad
- right
- wrong
- more
- less
- better
- best
- worse
- improved
- superior
- inferior
- advanced

Confident writers also make big claims:

They were an <u>instant</u> success.
They <u>swept</u> across the country.
They had <u>absolute</u> power.

and they often assume 'we' and 'you' and 'one' agree with them:

<u>We</u> can see their churches today, still standing after 1,000 years. In any conversation, <u>you</u> will hear Viking words that have been absorbed into the English language. If <u>one</u> could only travel back in time, the links would be clear to see.

In the following passage, find the words that convey:

a confidence
b judgements
c big claims
d agreement

Certainly they were cruel, efficient and terrifying invaders but there is no doubt that they made good farmers and strong-knit communities. The truth is that they were more advanced in every respect than the people they defeated. One has to admire them.

Try it

● Write two or three sentences that confidently describe the results of a survey about designer-label trainers.
● Write two or three sentences that confidently compare the latest CD, game or album with the one that came before it.

►► Test it

Write a paragraph of five or six sentences for a leaflet to shoppers explaining why you are closing the town centre to cars.

What you get marks for

Use of assertions (1 mark each)	up to 3 marks
Use of commands (1 mark each)	up to 2 marks
Use of confident expressions (1 mark each)	up to 3 marks
Overall effect is convincing and confident	up to 2 marks
Total	**10 marks**

ANSWERS

The assertions are b, c, e, g and h.

C. PUTTING ON THE STYLE

10. The formal voice

In this masterclass you will learn how to:

- write in a formal voice
- use passive verbs
- use precise vocabulary
- keep an even tone.

Introduction

The formal voice is the one you use with people in authority, or with people you don't know. It is:

- confident
- impersonal
- unemotional
- factual
- precise
- standard
- to the point.

You can use it to explain, complain, or make an agreement. It is useful when the truth is at stake. You might use it for:

- a job application
- a statement to the police
- a legal contract
- a letter of complaint
- a business letter or fax
- a manual
- a reference or rule book.

1. Using passive verbs

Formal language uses passive verbs.

Active verbs tell you who did what to whom.
Passive verbs start with the object and tell you what was done to it, and sometimes never even tell you who did it.

Active – We broke Mr Jay's window.
Passive – Mr Jay's window was broken.

Active – I trampled on the daffodils.
Passive – The daffodils had been trampled.

Like magic, the passive verb lets you off admitting who or what did it.

Spot the seven passive verbs:

> ## Appendectomy
>
> The patient is given a general anaesthetic. A small incision is made in the lower right abdomen. The appendix is then carefully and gently brought to the surface of the abdomen, clamped, tied off at the base and cut off. The stump is tied with a suture.

From *Family Health* ed. Tony Smith

Help ▶▶

Using the passive

- Start with the person or object that is on the receiving end of the verb – the victim, the thing that something happens to.
- The passive verb often has two parts, e.g. was punched, had fallen.
- If you want to, you can include the person who did it at the end, e.g. Stephen's hands were grabbed from behind *by Michael Russell*.

Compare:

Bullies
Michael Russell grabbed Stephen's hands from behind and held him fast while John Cross kicked at his knees until he slumped to the ground.

with:

Bullied
Stephen's hands were grabbed from behind and his knees were kicked until he slumped to the ground.

What difference does it make when you change the verbs from active to passive?

2. Using precise vocabulary

Notice the choice of words in the *Appendectomy* extract:

> **appendectomy**
>
> **incision**
>
> **abdomen**
>
> **suture**

Give the common words you would use for these terms.

In formal writing, aim for the most precise word. A doctor would not rely on the word *stitch* because it has other meanings. And expressions like *feeling sick* mean different things to different people. And some words are too vague. For example, a cut could be a deep wound, graze or an incision.

Spot the problem with the words:

> **poorly**
>
> **diet**
>
> **sore**
>
> **spots**

Precision

To be more precise you can:

- find a more accurate word
- give more detail
- add adjectives.

For example:
She's covered in spots.

↓

A rash of tiny yellow blisters extends over her arms and back.

Try it

Write a formal accurate description of a playground injury to enter in the school Accident Record Book.

3. Keeping an even tone

In stories, the tone varies with the events in the story. Sometimes it is tense, sometimes it is exciting and sometimes it is thoughtful. But in formal writing, the tone is even.

Compare:

> **Jay leaned against the mirror in the corner of the lift and watched the lift doors hiss and close. That was when the wave of numbness swept upwards and swallowed him. His throat stuck in the middle of swallowing and his heart rattled as the lift sighed and began to rise. Behind his nose a sickness mounted; his hands were rubber. Somewhere far away, a drum was banging: his heart panicked.**

with:

> **A panic attack is a brief period of acute anxiety, often dominated by an intense fear of dying or losing one's reason. The symptoms begin suddenly and usually include a sense of breathing difficulty, chest pains, palpitations, feeling light-headed and dizzy, sweating, trembling and faintness. Although unpleasant and frightening, panic attacks last for only a few minutes and cause no physical harm. Relaxation exercises may be of some help.**

- How does the writer of the first extract take the reader through the shifts of feeling in the panic attack?
- How does the writer of the second extract stop the reader going through the same shifts in feeling?

Write two contrasting paragraphs about an accident at the bend of a mountain road, in which a car crashes into the barrier and only just avoids a steep drop.

- Write one paragraph that describes it in a story and helps the reader to follow the shifts of feeling.
- Write another paragraph that describes it in a police report.

Keeping an even tone
- Keep to facts.
- Keep sentences a similar length.
- Use accurate words.
- Keep emotions out of it.

4. Formal writing

Here is an example of formal writing from a medical encyclopaedia:

Influenza

Influenza is a viral infection of the respiratory tract that causes fever, headache, muscle ache and weakness. It is spread by virus-infected droplets coughed or sneezed into the air. In all but the mildest cases, a person with influenza should rest in bed in a warm, well ventilated room. Analgesic drugs should be taken to relieve aches and pains and to reduce fever. Warm fluids soothe a sore throat and inhaling steam has a soothing effect on the lungs.

From *Family Health* ed. Tony Smith

- What features are typical of formal English?

Try it

Rewrite the following paragraph into formal language.

Head lice

Head lice love hair and they aren't fussy: long, short, straight, curly, clean, dirty – any hair will do! They can't fly, but they can crawl, and you catch them when you get close to someone who already has them. They feed on your blood by sucking at your scalp, leaving behind an itchy scab. If you look closely, you can see where they lay tiny hard white eggs on your hair. The eggs cling on with all their might and you can only shift them by combing hard with a fine comb and using a special shampoo that kills them.

▶▶ Test it))))

Use the following information to write an entry in a medical encyclopaedia that describes the plague under three headings:

What it is
The symptoms
The progress of the disease

Write only two sentences under each heading.

The plague

Also known as Yersona pestis

Also known as bubonic plague

Also known as The Black Death

25 million people died of it in the 1300s

Carried by fleas that live on rats

Fleas infect people when they bite

Can be spread by saliva when kissing or coughing

Fever starts three or four days later

Headache

Neck glands swell up

Cured by antibiotics

If not, big red sores appear in joints ('buboes')

What you get marks for

The vocabulary is factual and accurate	2 marks
The tone is even and unemotional	2 marks
Most sentences use passive verbs	2 marks
There are no personal pronouns (you, I or we)	1 mark
The overall effect is fluent and formal	3 marks
Total	**10 marks**

11. Plain clear writing

In this masterclass you will learn how to:

- be clear about what you want to say
- express yourself in plain language
- be direct.

Introduction

You mean to be clear but it comes out garbled. What goes wrong?

It may be that:

- You ramble because you haven't got it straight in your head yet.
- You know what you mean but you can't find the right words.
- You start saying it and then keep adding in and adding on.
- You tie yourself in knots trying to be too clever.
- You get stuck in the wrong style.

Example

Clear:

> **Placing an order**
> **Fill in the number of the product on the order form and hand it in at the till.**

Not clear:

> **For speedy and efficient processing of your order, our customer service managers (situated at till points around the store) will be pleased to receive the order form, of which there are several available at the catalogue points. Each item has an order number which should be entered accurately on the order form (6 digits) and forwarded to the customer service managers who will deal with customers in strict rotation.**

Discuss what makes this unclear.

The main problem is that the writer has told the customer how the system works instead of what to do. It is written as description instead of instruction. The style is not the best one to use.

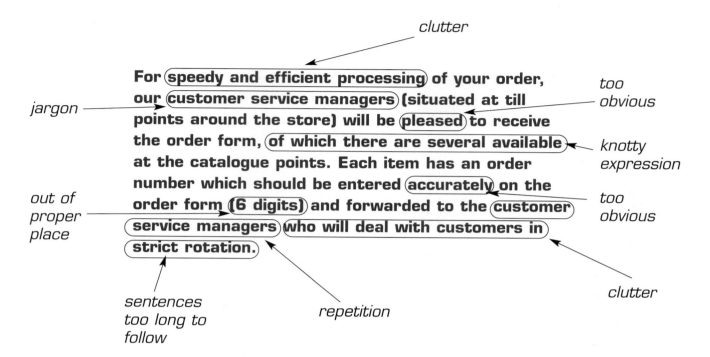

clutter

jargon

too obvious

knotty expression

too obvious

out of proper place

clutter

sentences too long to follow

repetition

For (speedy and efficient processing) of your order, our (customer service managers) (situated at till points around the store) will be (pleased) to receive the order form, (of which there are several available) at the catalogue points. Each item has an order number which should be entered (accurately) on the order form (6 digits) and forwarded to the (customer service managers) (who will deal with customers in strict rotation.)

Hot Tip ⏩

Think about the purpose

When you write, think who it is for and what it is for, and choose the best style before you start.

If you want to tell someone what to do

- Keep it short and simple so your readers can look up quickly from what they are doing to check they have it right.
- Say what to do at the start of the sentence and put the detail after.

If you want to make a point

- Make the point first.
- Back it up with arguments.
- Justify each argument.
- Explain your conclusion.

1. Diagnosing the problem

What is wrong with the language in these two texts?

1. From a story written by a pupil

He came in the door, smashed with splinters all over, falling on the floor, rolling over, grabbed his gun and pointed it at Wade. Wade pointed back. He shot him at point blank range. He looked around suspiciously but he was dead.

2. From a leaflet telling you how to assemble a chair

Maximum comfort can be obtained if the cushions are initially positioned in the recesses (at Point B on diagram A – see leaflet 'Fitment') and then adjusted to suit, and supplemented as necessary with additional Comfort Cushions (Ach.CC/02). Details on the website. Adjustable headrests (Ach.AH/03-05) are available as optional extras and can be purchased at the online Sales Site or via the Customer Careline (number on handycard, Mon–Fri 0830–1600) in Burgundy Plum, Vanilla or Tilth. Quote ref Ach.SO.57.

Discuss what makes plain clear writing and make a list of points.

Rewrite the two texts for clarity.

2. Simplifying your writing

Here are three ways to simplify your writing.

Say it directly

Indirect	Direct
Customers are advised that calls to the company are not chargeable.	Business calls are free.

De-clutter your sentences

They sell a lot of household goods such as bleach and bottle openers, as well as stationery including greeting cards, pens and school equipment, plus bread, butter, fruit and vegetables.

Cut out examples and wasted words:

They sell a lot of household goods such as bleach and bottle openers, as well as stationery including greeting cards, pens and school equipment, plus bread, butter, fruit and vegetables.

Or summarise:

They sell household goods, stationery and groceries.

Choose simpler words

excessive ➡ too much
deceased ➡ dead
cleansing bar ➡ soap

Try it

Make this notice friendly and easy to read by simplifying it.

Glebe Park
Regulations for the daytime use of this public space

1. For the security of younger users, residents are requested to close the access gate firmly on entry and exit.

2. Dog owners are advised that prosecutions will be enforced in the case of dogs committing offences including soiling of grass or borders, harassment of other users or excessive noise or disturbance.

3. Access is not permitted between the hours of 2030 and 0700.

4. Use of the junior play equipment is restricted to children aged 7 or below.

5. It is an offence to damage park flora or fixtures including benches, play equipment, litter bins and other fittings.

6. Discard all waste in the rubbish bins which are provided at various points in the park.

---

3. How to write clearly

1 Think about the **purpose** and the **needs** of the readers and decide on the best **style**.

2 Divide it up in your head.

3 Run through each paragraph in your head and separate out the points you want to make. The points might be actions.

4 Say each sentence fully in your head before you write it. If it is too complicated to hold in your head, you have two choices:

- Break it into two sentences.
- Be sure of its shape and how it will finish before you start writing.

Try it

- For the benefit of an alien, explain in three sentences how to serve a tennis ball.
- Think of four good arguments against after-school detentions and express them in a single sentence.
- Write two exciting sentences for a story in which your fishing boat is suddenly upturned by an unseen force and you have a narrow escape.

Test it

In pairs or threes, play the game **Squares** using a board of 6 x 6 dots. Once you are sure you know how to play, your test task is to explain how to play the game in four short paragraphs next to the diagrams. Rewrite Paragraph 1. Use the notes to write Paragraphs 2 and 3. Write Paragraph 4 yourself.

1. Introduction

This game is called squares and it needs two players or maybe more. There are dots on a board that you draw and you take turns to join the dots and make boxes and the one with most boxes is the person that wins. You have your own letter to write in the boxes.

2. How to play

1st player – join one dot to next dot – vertical or horizontal, not diagonal. Take turns.

3. Scoring points

How to make a box
Extra goes
Tips

4. How to win

What you get marks for

The introduction is short and simple	1 mark
There are no ambiguities in the introduction	1 mark
The points in the 'How to play' section are sensibly separated	1 mark
The 'How to play' section is clear	1 mark
The explanations in the 'Scoring points' section are clear	2 marks
The 'How to win' section is short, clear and simple	2 marks
The whole game is well explained so a non-player could follow it	2 marks
Total	**10 marks**

D. TELLING

12. Ways of telling

In this masterclass you will learn how to:

- choose and use different narrative approaches
- exploit time and pace
- make your writing more reflective and mature.

1. Different ways of telling

There are many different ways of telling.

Action – when you describe what people do.
Description – when you show what things look like.
Reflection – when you think about things.
Dialogue – when you give the words that people say.
Commentary – when the narrator comments directly on things.

The best writers move between them, choosing the best one for the moment.

Example

A church clock

The clock hung in an iron frame. It was all rods, cogs and wheels. It kept time twice. There was a drive to the hours and minutes and the pendulum, and a drive to the bell hammer. The bell was fixed, and the hour was struck on it. Both drives were weights held by two cables, each wound to a drum. The weights fitted in slots that ran down to the base of the tower.

Every week father cleaned and oiled the clock, and wound the weights back up. It took them a week to drop the height of the tower. He wound the cables with a key like a crank handle.

'She's getting two minutes,' said Father. 'It's this dry weather.'

From *The Aimer Gate* by Alan Garner

Each paragraph uses a different way of telling.
Work out which ones then check your answers on page 71.

2. Using time

The writer of the last extract spent most time on description because it is an unusual clock. He does what you would do if you were there: he looks at it and works out how it runs. The story pauses to make us 'look'. We are following his eyes.

Time in the *first* paragraph seems still: we are looking at a frozen moment in time, like looking at a photograph.

Time in the *second* paragraph moves as it does in a story. We follow what happens every week.

In the *third* paragraph we move in real time as Father speaks.

In real life you have to move in real time. One of the most powerful things a writer can do is to play with time. You can slow time down or rush through it.

Here is another example:

Climbing the church steeple

A twenty-nine stave ladder led to the clock chamber above. The ladder had its own rhythm, no whip or bend, no clattering extension.

Robert always stopped to watch when he was on the ladder. The pendulum came and went in the dim light, came and went. Through the trapdoor and past the platform the floor tiles were a long way off.

He climbed up, stepped sideways from the ladder to the planks of the chamber and put the baggin against the clock.

Here, everything was different again, and open.

From *The Aimer Gate* by Alan Garner

Work out:

- how the writer moves between different types of telling
- how time moves
- why the writer did it this way.

Find answers on page 71.

Try it

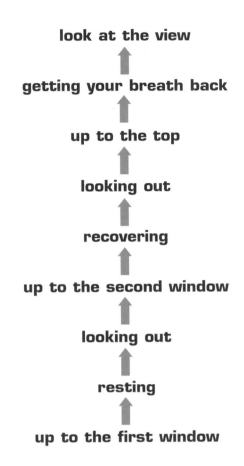

look at the view

⬆

getting your breath back

⬆

up to the top

⬆

looking out

⬆

recovering

⬆

up to the second window

⬆

looking out

⬆

resting

⬆

up to the first window

- Imagine a flight of stairs up a tower.
- Imagine what hard work it is to climb the stairs.
- Imagine stopping for breath at the first window and looking at the view.
- Go higher and stop again at the second window.
- Go to the top and take in the view.

Write about your experience in a few paragraphs. Do it in sections, shifting between action, reflection and description at each stage.

Hot Tip ▶▶

Drama in the head

A good tip for getting the pace and detail right is to imagine the event happening to you in real time.

- Find a quiet place and close your eyes.
- If there is nowhere to go, gaze at a blank sheet of paper or close your ears.
- Imagine each section of the climb in real time, stopping to write at the end of each section.

3. Using reflection

- Most people write action and dialogue.
- Many people write commentary.
- Some people use description.
- But few people use reflection.

Description and reflection are important because they are the thinking and feeling bits of the story. They slow down the pace and make you think. A story is more sophisticated if it has them.

Compare:

Bullies (1)

I was tiptoeing across the porch when some kids started chanting. I could hear thuds and cries as well. Somebody was getting beaten up.

I crept to the doorway and peeped out and it was Scott, surrounded by all these kids. He fell down and they started kicking him. He'd spoken up for me when Simon Pritchard kicked me in class, so they'd turned on him.

I turned and ran back, heading for the staffroom. As I crossed the hall, Mr Kilroy came out of the PE store and yelled 'Walk, girl, don't run!'

'Please sir,' I gasped, 'there's a gang beating a kid up in the yard.'

He didn't hang about. 'Show me,' he rapped, so I ran and he followed. When the kids saw him coming they ran.

From *Abomination* by Robert Swindells

With:

Bullies (2)

I was tiptoeing across the porch, listening, when some kids started chanting. I could hear thuds and cries as well, and I knew somebody was getting beaten up.

I nearly went back to the toilets. I don't know why I didn't. Something stopped me, that's all I know. I crept to the doorway and peeped out and it was Scott, surrounded by all these kids. As I watched, he fell down and they started kicking him and I knew it was my fault. He'd spoken up for me when Simon Pritchard kicked me in class, so they'd turned on him.

I didn't know what to do. If I was brave, I'd have charged at them, punching and kicking to rescue my friend, but I'm not so I turned and ran back, heading for the staffroom. As I crossed the hall, Mr Kilroy came out of the PE store and yelled 'Walk, girl, don't run!'

'Please sir,' I gasped, 'there's a gang beating a kid up in the yard.'

I don't like Mr Kilroy because he's sarky to kids who're useless at PE but give him his due – he didn't hang about. 'Show me,' he rapped, so I ran and he followed. When the kids saw him coming they ran like rabbits.

From *Abomination* by Robert Swindells

Bullies 1 contains only action and dialogue.
Bullies 2 adds description and reflection.
What is better about the second version?

Now write two extra paragraphs about what happens next. Include equal amounts of action, dialogue, reflection and description.

ANSWERS

A church clock

1 Description   2 Action   3 Dialogue

Climbing the church steeple

1 Description   3 Action
2 Reflection   4 Reflection

Time moves as the boy moves up the bell tower, and stops as he stops to look about, to rest and to think.

▶ Test it

You have slipped from a mountain path onto a rock ledge. Your task is to describe in one side of writing how you save your own life by making the dangerous climb from the ledge back to the path.

Hot Tip ▶

- Plan it out first. Break it into sections.
- Most of the sections will be action.
- Build in reflection (e.g. stopping to rest).
- Build in description (e.g. looking around).

What you get marks for

For breaking the writing into clear sections	2 marks
1 mark for every time you add reflection	up to 3 marks
1 mark for every time you add description	up to 3 marks
For the overall effect	2 marks
Total	**10 marks**

D. TELLING

13. Telling by showing

In this masterclass you will learn how to:

- show rather than inform
- suggest character
- use symbols.

Introduction

Sometimes it is best to tell your readers what they need to know because it's quick, easy and direct. You can give them the facts because that's what they need.

But if you want them to get personally involved, then **show** them rather than **tell** them. Let them work it out for themselves.

Example

Here is a writer showing us a man and letting us work him out for ourselves:

> Ron Garnet, Chief Development Engineer for Cogent Electronics, clicked the button on the remote control. The last graph disappeared, the screen went black and the teak door that thirty minutes before had slid noiselessly open, slid noiselessly closed. Garnet pressed the button under the table. The curtains in the window waltzed to a rhythm of low click–clicks and the New England sunlight flooded in.

From *The Stream* by Brian Clarke

We are told some facts: his job, for example. But we know much more without being told: that he is wealthy, privileged and American. We guess he must work for a large, successful hi-tech company. We are not told all this. We work most of it out from the clues.

- Find the clues.

Try it

1 In three sentences, describe someone sitting at an office desk in a small, struggling, old-fashioned car sales business in America. Don't tell any of this, but do show it. Make sure there are enough clues to work it out.

2 In one sentence, describe a man who has been rich in the past but is now down on his luck. He is vain and doesn't like to admit that he has come down in the world. Show rather than tell.

3 In one sentence, describe a woman who is very rich but lacks taste and was once poor. Show rather than tell.

Telling by showing

Clues might include:

- what people wear, e.g. overalls
- how people behave, e.g. wiping nose on sleeve
- the vocabulary, e.g. sidewalk = American
- the setting, e.g. aging furniture
- the adjectives, e.g. gloomy
- the use of suggestive detail, e.g. bare light bulbs
- the way they speak, e.g. he drawled
- details of the face or expression, e.g. leering
- the use of telling verbs, e.g. she snapped, he peered.

1. Looking from the outside in

Writers often tell us what the characters in a story are thinking and feeling, but sometimes they don't and sometimes they can't, perhaps because the narrator is a person in the story.

There would not be much story if we knew what all the characters were up to. There would be no mysteries to unravel. Instead, writers give us clues about how the characters are feeling or get them to speak their mind.

Example

They were driving into Garmouth before Mother said defensively:

'You do remember Prudie, don't you?'

'Course I remember Prudie,' snapped Anne. 'She did look after me until I was eight.'

'I've seen her since,' said Mother. 'She's changed. Her hair's gone grey.' Mother made it sound like the end of the world; for Mother it would have been.

'But I'm sure she'll look after you,' added Mother. 'Like she always did.'

'Yes,' said Anne, flatly.

'I'm grateful to Prudie for taking you, of course. But I'll not pretend she's ideal.'

From *The Watch House* **by Robert Westall**

Working out how people feel

Look for:

- behaviour that gives away their thoughts and feelings
- body language – expression, posture, movements
- adjectives and adverbs that reveal their state of mind
- how you would feel in the same situation
- clues in the conversation.

There are several clues that tell us that Mother is quite well off – she owns a car, she is *Mother* not *Mum*, she once hired a nanny. She is a snob, too – can you find two clues?

What can you work out about:

- why they are going to Garmouth?
- how Anne is feeling?
- how Mother is feeling?

Think about it

Think of three things that might reveal:

- feelings of impatience
- feelings of guilt
- class background
- age, even without seeing the face
- the country in which the events take place
- whether the setting is the city or the country.

Try it

1   In three sentences, describe a man waiting for someone to pass him stolen goods. Try to show that he is:
- impatient
- nervous
- waiting well beyond the time he expected
- afraid of being recognised.

2   In three sentences, describe meeting a businessman who introduces you to a young woman claiming she is his business partner. Without saying so directly, make your reader understand that this is a lie.

3   In two sentences, describe someone who looks perfectly ordinary but who will later turn out to be the villain. Put something into the description that will warn the reader that there's something shifty about this person. This must not be anything too obvious.

2. Using symbols

Another way of helping the reader to work it out is to use objects and events to set the mood or suggest what it all means.

Example

A secret arrival at a military airfield

It was a filthy night and in the roar of the engines and the spray the vast aircraft threw up, Longsworth almost missed the two figures running out from under one of the huge wings, coming at his open-topped Land Rover at a dead run and slinging their kitbags into the back before climbing on board. Longsworth had started to introduce himself but as he did so the plane's engines rose to a pitch and it turned in a fast circle and immediately began to taxi back to the main apron. Longsworth watched, puzzled as it began its take-off run and then it was gone as if it had never been there. He turned to look at his two passengers and opened his mouth to speak but something stopped him. He started the engine and began to drive back towards the small empty stores building that had been requisitioned as a place for the two men to wait.

From *The Sirius Crossing* by John Creed

The **weather** is a common symbol. Here it is a 'filthy night'. It is a symbol of bad and secret events going on under cover of darkness.

There are several other examples:

- the men running out from *under the wing* of the aircraft
- the men move in a *dead run*
- Longsworth can't introduce himself because *his words are drowned* by aircraft noise.

Find some more examples, and say what it all suggests.

Try it

Write the paragraph called **A secret departure at a military airfield** in which the two airmen catch another plane later that night and Longsworth is sure they are flying off on a deadly mission.

You can read John Creed's original on the next page.

▶▶ Test it ⟩⟩⟩

Write the first three or four paragraphs of a spy novel.

Dana, a secret agent, is waiting anxiously in a city square one evening for another spy to contact her. She doesn't know who it is, and it is getting late. Finally, someone arrives, but Dana can tell something is not right...

Show the events rather than tell them. Your readers must be able to work it all out for themselves.

What you get marks for

For communicating the following without saying so directly:

• that she is waiting	1 mark
• that she is anxious	1 mark
• that the other person is late	1 mark
• that she doesn't know who it is	1 mark
• that she is a secret agent	1 mark
• that something is wrong about the person who arrives	1 mark
For making an overall effect that is mysterious and tense	2 marks
Overall effect is not over the top	2 marks
Total	**10 marks**

ANSWERS

John Creed's original

Without a word, the two Americans slid over the side of the jeep and ran towards the plane. Longsworth watched them go. A hatch opened in the side of the fuselage and the two men threw themselves over the lip of it. As the plane turned in the apron, Longsworth felt a shiver running down his spine. There was something about this small black plane that stirred irrational fears in him. As it taxied away into the dark, he remembered the story of Charon, the ferryman who ferried the dead across the River Styx into the underworld.

From *The Sirius Crossing* by John Creed

D. TELLING

14. Definition

In this masterclass you will learn how to:

- define character
- define places
- make defining statements.

A dictionary *defines* words. With a camera or a television, *definition* means getting the picture sharp and focused. A *defining* moment is one in which the true nature of something is revealed. A *definitive* answer is a clear and final answer. This unit is about definition in writing: getting at the true nature of something sharply and clearly.

1. Defining character

Pay attention to the way characters are drawn. Writers can use description to tell the reader what lies inside the character. An example:

> In later years he sprouted a moustache – looked after with fanatical care – which suited him. His lips were pinched and thin and his voice escaped through them like steam through the apertures of a whistling kettle.

From *The Chip-Chip Gatherers* by Shiva Naipaul

From this extract, we find out what the man looks like, but it also tells us something about the nature of man. It tells us he was obsessive and had pent-up feelings. The writer suggests this by:

- telling us directly: he uses the word *fanatical*
- choosing verbs that capture his high energy: *sprouted* rather than *grew*, *escaped* rather than *spoke*
- association: *pinched* and *thin* lips are associated with mean, repressed people
- using simile: comparing him with a boiling kettle.

Analyse this (1)

> **May**
>
> The doorbell rang. May, whose month it was, did not look very spring-like, nor would she ever look very summery, no matter how hot it might become. She would change her small modest navy felt hat for a small navy straw.

From *Bag and Baggage* by Judy Allen

- The writer defines May's character in two ways. What are they?
- Look at the list in the Help box. Which techniques does this writer use?

Describing people

To show what people are like:
- concentrate on character rather than appearance
- focus on the most important thing about their character
- choose only their most telling feature or two features
- choose exact adjectives and nouns
- think of them doing things rather than still like a portrait
- picture them doing something typical
- choose verbs that tell you something about their character
- compare with them with something or someone else
- use a simile or a metaphor
- use a style of language that reflects the character of the person
- place them in a setting that reflects their character.

Analyse this (2)

Read the following description and decide how it defines the person and what techniques are used to do it.

A Welsh preacher

His voice knows only two colours: the bright yellow of a peaceful sun, and the threatening red of hell. Only two sounds: the whisper of a branch moved by the wind, and the thundering of an empty barrel falling downstairs. His hands know only two movements: the gentle movement of reaching for a flower, and the whirling of mill-sails in a storm.

From *Related Twilights* by Josef Herman

Try it

Think of a well-known person or a character on TV, but keep the name secret. Picture him or her in action. Work out his or her defining features. Write three sentences that show what he or she is like.

Take turns to read aloud your sentences and see if others can guess the person. If the guess is right, pinpoint the exact detail that gives it away.

2. Defining places

Describing a place is not so different from describing a person. The key is finding its defining feature. An example:

> **A deserted camp**
>
> We reached the rusty wire fence which surrounded the camp. The gates were open and we drove in. Liam went narrow-eyed when he saw the camp. The ghostly shapes of the buildings looming out of the mist, the sense of a once-thriving place now deserted, weeds growing through the tarmac, some of the prefabs toppled by the harsh Atlantic wind. It was a strange, moody, unsettling place and we caught its atmosphere, tendrils of fog floating past the windscreen.
>
> **From *The Sirius Crossing* by John Creed**

- Find two examples of the writer defining the feel of the place directly.
- Now find several details that contribute to the 'deserted' feel.
- The story is about soldiers finding a place to have a showdown with the enemy. They are in danger. Find three details that hint at danger.

Try it

Think of a museum at night when everyone has gone. Think of the objects in their cases. Think of the silence. Think of the dark.

Decide what it is that defines the place. Perhaps it is a precious object, or an idea about exhibits when no one looks at them, or something scary about things that are no longer used.

Write no more than four sentences of description that define the place.

Possible opening lines:

The clock strikes midnight, but...
As time crawls by, the shadows...
In their glass cases, the...

3. Defining statements

In a defining statement, the writer works up to a point of principle, and states an insight or truth.

> The best day of my life was the day I was presented with the buff-coloured beret of the SAS. I had just completed the selection for one of the Regiment's two territorial units, and was immensely proud of what I had achieved. I still am. Like selection for the regular unit, it involves months of back-breaking legwork and culminates in a gruelling fortnight in the Brecon Beacons, with an overall attrition rate of ninety per cent. For me the toil was infinitely worthwhile, because I believe that the SAS beret symbolises something rare in our society. It cannot be bought, inherited, or acquired by privilege. It has to be earned.

From *The Real Bravo Two Zero* by Michael Asher

This extract falls into three parts:

1 When the writer tells the story of getting the beret.

2 When he explains about the training.

3 When he says what it means to him.

- Find the beginning and end of each section.

- Notice the move from the particular to the general and then to the abstract.

- Also notice the move from the past to the present tense.

- Notice how forceful the last two lines are because they are short and use repetition and feel different from the everyday factual details that went before.

Help ▶▶

Defining statements

Defining statements are moments of insight or truth. They sound like proverbs. They are often:

- short and simple
- direct
- abstract
- written in the present tense
- summing up
- at the end or right in the middle
- built up from the particular to the general.

▶▶ Test it ▶▶▶

Imagine a person – real or imaginary – standing in a place that reflects his or her character.

Write no more than five or six sentences describing this person and then sum up how you feel about him or her. Finish with a defining statement.

An example is given below:

When my mam came home to us

Then, exactly on the hour, Mam comes walking over the bridge in her long coat. She's by herself, walking along at her own pace like she just happens to be there. I know she's watching for us. She's squinting and staring ahead, to make sure he's brought us to where he's supposed to. It looks wrong, Mam just standing by herself. She stands in the middle, right in the middle.

From *Strange Boy* by Paul Magrs

What you get marks for

Choice of telling details	2 marks
Use of words that hint or suggest the character	2 marks
Use of comparison, e.g. simile, metaphor	1 mark
Moving from the specific to the general	1 mark
Writing a good defining statement	1 mark
Overall impact of the description	3 marks
Total	**10 marks**

15. *Planning writing in the test*

In this masterclass you will learn how to:

- get a fix on the test question
- plan your answer
- plan your time.

1. Getting a fix on the question

In these three titles, look for the key word that tells you how to go about the answer:

Write a review of the play *Macbeth*.

Write an introduction to the play *Macbeth*.

Write a summary of the play *Macbeth*.

How should each piece of writing be different?

Find an answer on page 90.

Discuss the difference between the following:

Express your views about cloning.

Explore your views about cloning.

Explain your views about cloning.

Describe the poverty trap.

Discuss the poverty trap.

Debate the poverty trap.

What would you do differently in each case?

Help ▶▶

Key word in a question

- The key word is likely to be a noun or verb about *a type of writing*.
- Work out who you are writing for – a theatre audience? a parent?
- Work out what use it will be to them – to make a decision? to advise?
- Work out what the tone should be – reassuring? thoughtful?
- Work out what the style should be – simple? direct?
- Work out what role you are in – critic? friend? guide?

Say three things you would need to bear in mind in writing for the reader in these tasks:

1   Write a leaflet for small children about visiting the doctor.

2   Write a review of a new computer battle game for a teenage magazine.

3   Write a letter asking parents to send their milk bottle tops and silver foil into school to raise money for a local charity.

Consider the reader

Consider the needs of the reader and adapt your style to suit.

Decide:

- tone
- formality
- simplicity
- length
- level of detail.

2. Making a quick plan

This is a two or three minute job. You need it most of all if you are the kind of person who:

- runs out of steam when you write
- runs out of time when you write
- gets lost when you write.

Make a quick plan for each of these questions. You have exactly three minutes for each one. Plan in single words or notes and in pencil. Use a diagram that fits the type of writing. Use the table opposite to help.

1   Discuss the argument for banning smacking.

2   Write a guide to a visitor with one hour to spend seeing the most interesting things in your locality.

3   Write an informative leaflet about your class for a new pupil joining it.

Keep your plans for the next section.

Question	Planning
Explain a process	Use a flow chart
Debate an issue	Use for and against columns For | Against

Explain an issue or opinion	List the points and gather examples, ideas, or details around them
	
	1 Point 1
	   • Ideas & examples
	2 Point 2
	   • Ideas & examples
	3 Point 3
	   • Ideas & examples

Explore a topic	Use a star chart
Write a narrative	Use a writing structure **1** Establish context **2** Introduce problem **3** Intensify it **4** Complicate it **5** Build up to climax **6** Climax **7** Adjust to new situation **8** Conclude
Any question that completely stumps you	List 5 points to make and put them in order **1** **2** **3** **4** **5**

3. Timing the writing

Your plan should divide up the work. Match the plan against the time available. Work out the time you can give to each section.

Example

Suppose you have 35 minutes left to write a leaflet for children about safety in the kitchen. You have this plan:

1   **Introduction – cooking is fun – but need to be safe – use common sense**

2   **Ovens & rings – hot – pan handles – gas – flames – matches**

3   **Water – slippery floor – hot tap – getting wet – electricity**

4   **Cupboards – take care getting things out – high cupboards – knives**

5   **Cans & bottles – check labels – breakages**

6   **Conclusion – ask adults to help – have fun**

That's 5 minutes for each section, and 5 minutes left over to check for obvious mistakes.

1	**Introduction**	**5 minutes**
2	**Ovens & rings**	**5 minutes**
3	**Water**	**5 minutes**
4	**Cupboards**	**5 minutes**
5	**Cans & bottles**	**5 minutes**
6	**Conclusion**	**5 minutes**
7	**Checking**	**5 minutes**
Total		*35 minutes*

- Discuss what to do if you find yourself 10 minutes behind when you get to **Cupboards**. (You expected to have 20 minutes left at this point but you only have 10.)

- Discuss what to do if you're on time but realise at **Cans & bottles** that you've forgotten to cover electrical equipment.

- What if you didn't remember electrical equipment until you were checking at the end?

Try it

Time your planned question for these times:

- Smacking   35 minutes
- Visitor to the locality   25 minutes
- Guide for a new pupil   30 minutes

4. Preparing starters

This is important if you tend to dry up or finish badly. It's also good if you tend to forget paragraphs.

Before you start writing, compose the opening line of each section. It will get you into the style and the mood and it will support you when you start to flag.

Example

Introduction	**The kitchen is a place for fun, but it can also be...**
Ovens & rings	**Most kitchen accidents happen around the oven...**
Water	**Water may not seem like a danger in the kitchen, but...**
Cupboards	**A quick look around your cupboards will tell you...**
Cans & bottles	**Anything that can break, fall or spill may be...**
Conclusion	**If you follow these simple rules, you will be safe...**

Try it

Write sentence starters for your three titles.

Test it

Plan your answer to the following question in 10 minutes, showing the plan, the timing and the sentence starters:

> Argue the case for electronic identity tags for all citizens at birth.
>
> Total time allowed: 35 mins

What you get marks for

The plan has an introduction and conclusion	1 mark
The plan contains three or more clear points in favour of tagging	3 marks
The times are sensibly distributed	2 marks
The starters give a good sense of how the writing will develop	4 marks
Total	**10 marks**

ANSWERS

Planning the *Macbeth* answer:

The key words here are *review*, *introduction* and *summary*.

- A **review** is an opinion about the play written for someone deciding whether to see it or not. It will say what the play is about and who is in it, and then say what was strong or weak about it and make a recommendation. It doesn't give the ending away.

- An **introduction** is written to prepare someone who is about to see the play. It gives background information and points up the main themes, even the big issue in it, but it doesn't give the ending away.

- A **summary** gives a brief account of the whole plot.

16. Composing paragraphs

In this masterclass you will learn how to:

- compose paragraphs
- link paragraphs.

Introduction

Writing is divided into paragraphs for two reasons:

- to show the reader how the text is organised
- to tell the reader when there has been a change of topic, time, place or point of view.

There are no fixed rules about paragraphs, but in school it is common to see:

- three to four paragraphs on each page
- three to five sentences in each paragraph
- the first sentence in each paragraph pointing out the shift in time, topic or point of view
- the last sentence in a paragraph rounding up and sometimes pointing the way to the next paragraph.

The most important decision about a paragraph is how to organise its content. Sometimes it is obvious, for example in stories that tell things in the order in which they happen. It is harder with factual information and argument because there is no fixed order.

Here are some common ways of organising material in a paragraph:

1. In order of event

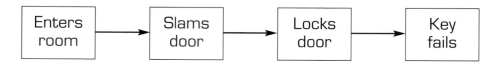

Martin staggered into the room, twisted and looked back. The stairhead at the far end of the corridor gaped wider. He was sure of it. He slammed the door shut, felt a key under his fingers and turned it. The lock shut to, but the key fell to the floor.

From *The Key* **by John Gordon**

2. Making a point

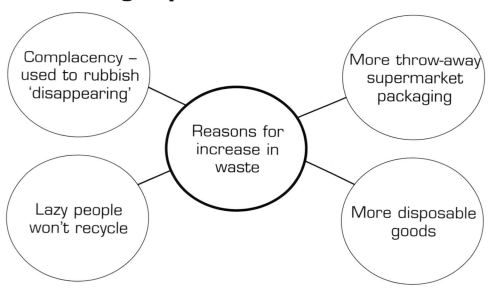

Today people throw away more belongings than ever before because when goods wear out it's cheaper to buy a replacement than to spend time and money mending it. Supermarket packaging is thrown away as soon as the item is opened at home. People won't take the time to compost, re-use or recycle their waste: they have got used to it disappearing as if by magic once a week.

3. Categorising information

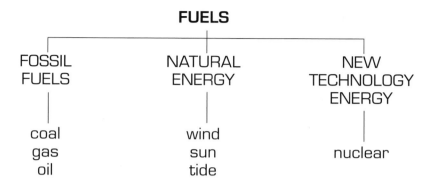

There are different types of fuel. Fossil fuels such as coal, oil and gas are taken from the earth and burnt to release their energy. More recently there has been a return to the natural energy captured from the wind, sun and tide using windmills, solar panels and wave machines. New technology has enabled us to create nuclear energy by splitting atoms.

4. By order of importance

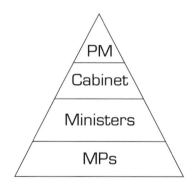

The Prime Minister is the head of government. He or she is assisted by the cabinet, a group of MPs known as secretaries of state who run the different departments such as education and health. Each of them is assisted by ministers who help them to run their departments. Other MPs are known as backbenchers.

The important thing is to have an **organising principle** for your paragraph. This means having a mental picture of its structure. You decide in what order you will say the things you want to say.

What is the organising principle behind each of these paragraphs?

Suddenly, I was jarred awake when the door slammed open. 'It's the alligators, come quick!' Steve was yelling. I leapt out of bed and started scrambling for my clothes with no idea what was going on. 'Just put your clothes on and hurry!' Steve shouted over his shoulder as he ran out the door. I pounded on Dawn's door as I laced up my shoes and she dutifully raced after me in her pyjamas as we hurried towards the alligator enclosure.

As we got to the outer safety fence, I couldn't believe my eyes. Locked together in mortal combat were our two female alligators, aptly named the Fang Sisters. Their jaws were clamped down on each other's head in some sort of dispute. Their small peglike teeth were even puncturing skull and there was blood everywhere. Obstinate as bulldogs, they were not letting go! It would be hours before the staff would start arriving and these girls were busy trying to pull each other's heads off right now.

From *The Crocodile Hunter* by Steve and Terri Irwin

Try it

1. Twins' birthday party

The twins Jez and Jon have an argument about their joint birthday party:

Jez	*Jon*
Eat at Pizza Paradise	**Barbeque in garden**
Ice disco	**Film at home**
Cake & candles	**Fireworks**
Sleepover – 3 friends	**Tent in garden**
Midnight feast	**Ghost stories at midnight**

Write a paragraph describing a compromise plan for the party. What will be the organising principle for the paragraph?

2. City visit

Write a paragraph for a tourist visiting the sights of the capital city. Think of at least five places to see. What will be the organising principle for the paragraph?

Welcome to the capital city! Enjoy the best sights by...

3. Packing list

Use this list to organise a paragraph about what you should remember to take on holiday. What will be the organising principle for the paragraph?

Jeans	Cash	Towels
Tops	Passport	First aid kit
T-shirts	Books to read	Pen and notebook
Socks	Bats & ball	Umbrella
Underwear	Mobile phone	Swimming costume
Sponge bag	Snacks for journey	Holdall
Sun-tan cream	Sweets	Box of tissues
Brush	Drinks for journey	Fruit
Trainers	Addresses	Small radio
Camera	Map	
Spare film	Guidebook	

▶▶ Test it)))

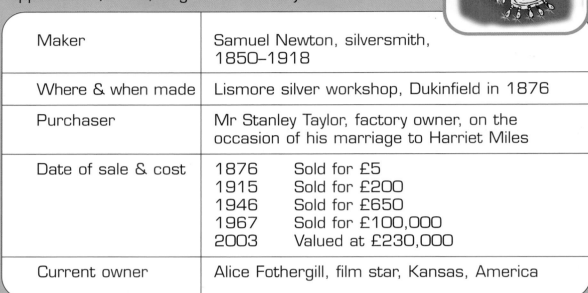

Use the information to write an article about the Newton Necklace in four paragraphs covering its appearance, value, origins and history.

Maker	Samuel Newton, silversmith, 1850–1918
Where & when made	Lismore silver workshop, Dukinfield in 1876
Purchaser	Mr Stanley Taylor, factory owner, on the occasion of his marriage to Harriet Miles
Date of sale & cost	1876 Sold for £5 1915 Sold for £200 1946 Sold for £650 1967 Sold for £100,000 2003 Valued at £230,000
Current owner	Alice Fothergill, film star, Kansas, America

1876	Made for Stanley Taylor as a gift to his new wife Harriet
1915	Harriet dies. Necklace sold to James Tasker
1925	Necklace stolen from Tasker safe
1928	Necklace recovered in police raid & returned to owner
1945	James dies in war
1946	Necklace sold by his widow to raise money
1967	Bought at auction for £100,000 by mystery buyer
2003	Spotted on neck of film star Alice Fothergill

What you get marks for

For breaking the writing into four clear paragraphs	1 mark
For starting each paragraph helpfully (0.5 mark each)	2 marks
For making clear links between each paragraph (0.5 mark each)	2 marks
For organising the information in each paragraph sensibly (1 mark each)	4 marks
For the overall effect	1 mark
Total	**10 marks**

17. Checking

In this masterclass you will learn how to:

- watch out for your own common errors
- check your work
- make neat corrections.

1. Knowing your own weak spots

Everyone makes mistakes when they rush. Use this list to find your own most common mistakes.

Common errors include:

☐ Forgetting to put in paragraphs
☐ Misspelling words that have soundalikes, e.g. of/have, there/their
☐ Certain spelling rules, e.g. when to change Y to IES in plurals
☐ Putting in commas instead of full stops when you rush
☐ Spending too long on the first section
☐ Running out of time
☐ Apostrophes – missing them out
☐ Apostrophes – putting them in where they don't belong
☐ Getting the commas and capitals wrong in speech punctuation
☐ Untidy handwriting
☐ Wandering away from the margin
☐ Retelling the story instead of answering the question
☐ Forgetting to back up your points with evidence such as examples
☐ Not explaining yourself because it seems obvious
☐ Writing vague or general answers
☐ Saying what you think instead of discussing what you think

2. Keeping an eye on errors

Think of a way to remember your most common mistakes.

For example:

PARAGRAPHS + **A**POSTROPHES + **TH**ERE/**TH**EIR
= **PATH**

Write it at the top of the answer paper.

Look at it as you are writing and it will help you to avoid errors.

Help Lindsay to think of a way to remember this set of errors:

1   Forgets to give examples.

2   Puts **of** instead of **have** in could have, should have, etc.

Make up a way of remembering your own common errors.

3. A checking routine

Check for the common mistakes noted at the top of the page.

Then check for other mistakes by reading through quickly.

If you are short of time, check the sections that gave you most trouble.

4. Making neat corrections

1. Correcting a small mistake

Don't make small mistakes worse by making a big correction. Capital letter and spelling mistakes should be corrected with little fuss.

Put the correction line straight through the letter and write the correct version overhead.

> a   m
> Wood is a vers|tile and long-lasting ~~Material~~.

Neat corrections

If you find mistakes, correct them using as little ink as possible.

- **Don't** scribble out.
- **Don't** squeeze new words in small spaces.
- Cross out using a single line made with a ruler.

2. Adding in a short correction

Use this insertion mark   where you wish to add something. Write the new words in the margin where there is more space. Put an insertion mark before them.

> Settlers used wood to build houses, and cleared trees for farming. They also used it ~~for lots of everyday things~~. Gradually the forests dwindled and then they disappeared.

> ⋏ as a construction material for a host of everyday items

3. Longer additions

Put longer additions at the end so that they don't spoil your whole page. You can do this by using a sign such as an asterisk or number that refers the examiner to the end of the writing.

F. NOTES

18. Notes to the pupil

The chapter lists the most common problems with writing, and suggests ideas for dealing with them.

1. Have a plan you can hold in your head

Example 1: A piece of personal writing

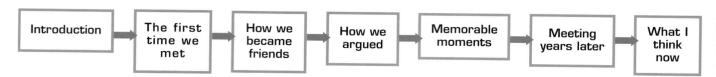

| Introduction | → | The first time we met | → | How we became friends | → | How we argued | → | Memorable moments | → | Meeting years later | → | What I think now |

Example 2: A guide to an exhibition

EXHIBITION GUIDE	
Exhibit 1	Exhibit 2
Exhibit 3	Exhibit 4
Exhibit 5	Exhibit 6

Example 3: A history essay

Introduction
↓
Causes

| Cause 1 | Cause 2 | Cause 3 | Cause 4 | Cause 5 |

Overview
↓
Conclusion

2. Stuck for ideas?
Use a planning shape to get ideas flowing

For and against columns

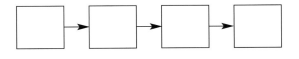

Star chart

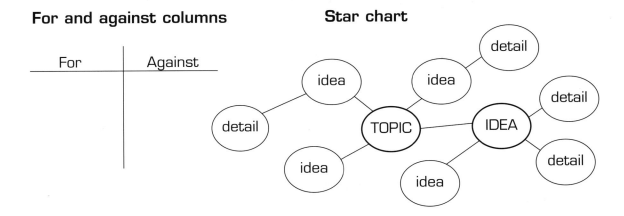

Flow chart

Grid

	Feature 1	Feature 2	Feature 3
Subject 1			
Subject 2			
Subject 3			

Never comes out right?

Rehearse the sentences in your head.

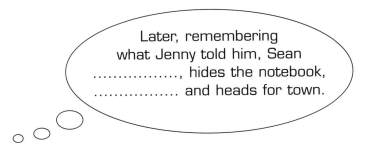

Later, remembering what Jenny told him, Sean ...., hides the notebook, ... and heads for town.

If the sentence is too long to remember, at least know how it will end. Consider breaking it up into two sentences.

3. Sounds flat?
Vary the way you start your sentences

Try starting with an adverb:

> <u>Slowly</u> he begins to think there is something wrong.

Or an adjective:

> <u>Talented, beautiful</u> Emma realises she is out of luck at last.

Or with a verb:

> <u>Returning</u> home, she has a sense that every good thing in her life is over.

Or a preposition:

> <u>Beyond</u> the gate, something has stirred in the darkness.

4. Replace some dull verbs with powerful verbs

Example:

> slithers   gliding
> The creature ~~draws~~ closer to the house, ~~moving~~ on a trail of sticky slime.

5. Replace some general nouns with strong specific nouns

Example:

> porch   slick
> The creature slithers closer to the ~~house~~, gliding on a ~~trail~~ of
> mucus
> sticky ~~slime~~.

6. Looks untidy? Line up and leave space

Even the worst handwriting looks better if you stick to the margin and leave a space round each answer.

Before:

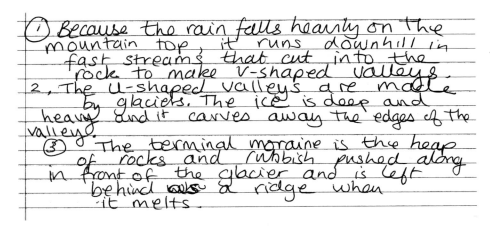

After:

1. Because the rain falls heavily on the mountain, it runs downhill in fast streams that cut into the rock to make V-shaped valleys.

2. The U-shaped valleys are made by glaciers. The ice is deep and heavy, and carves away the edges of the valley.

3. The terminal moraine is the heap of rocks and rubbish pushed along at the front of the glacier and is left behind as a ridge when it melts.

7. Horrible handwriting? Tidy up with six simple rules

1 Slope it all in the same direction (pencil in lines if you have to).

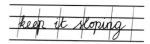

2 Make all the tails the same.

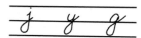

3 Keep it on the line.

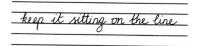

4 Change to a fountain pen with a thick nib.

5 Keep the small letters all the same height.

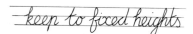

6 Change your worst letters one at a time for a week at a time.

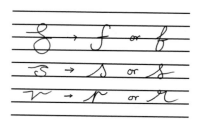

Try sticking to rule 1 for the first week.

Try sticking to rules 1 and 2 for the second week.

Try sticking to rules 1, 2 and 3 for the third week.

And so on...

Another way of dealing with poor handwriting is to learn a new style.

Choose one that is most different from the one you use now. Even if you never use it at speed, it will do for best. Here are three:

Recommended by the National Literacy Strategy:

a b c d e f g h i j
k l m n o p q r s t
u v w x y z

The Lucinda Sans font:

a b c d e f g h i j
k l m n o p q r s t
u v w x y z

A looped style so you can join up every letter without taking your pen off the paper:

a b c d e f g
h i j k l m n
o p q r s t
u v w x y z

8. Spelling's a nightmare? Learn the top 5 rules, 50 common words and top tips for learning

Top five rules

1 Plurals

Most plurals just add S.

Some words add ES because they end in a hissing, shushing or buzzing sound. The ES creates an extra syllable.

marsh – marshes	fizz – fizzes
bunch – bunches	cross – crosses

2 Doubling

Why one T in *writing* but two in *written*?

Why one N in *dining* but two in *dinner*?

Here's the trick: listen to the vowel just before it.

- If it's a long vowel (one that says its own name), use a single letter.
- If it's a short vowel, use double letters.

3 Adding prefixes

Just add prefixes. They never change the word.

dis + appear = disappear   dis + satisfied = dissatisfied

The only reason there are two Ss in *dissatisfied* is because the word *satisfied* already starts with an S.

4 Adding suffixes

Most suffixes can just be added with no changes to the original word, but watch out for:

Words ending in consonant + Y, e.g. *pity*

- Change Y to I if you add a suffix, e.g. pitiful, pitied, pitiless.
- But avoid having two Is together if you add a suffix starting with I such as ING e.g. pitying, not pitiing.

Words ending in consonant + E

- Keep the E in most cases.
- But drop it if the suffix starts with a vowel as it would put two vowels next to each other that don't belong, e.g. bore + ing = boring, not boreing.

5   Take care when two vowels sit together

IE – most common, e.g. thief.

EI – after C, e.g. receive or when it sounds like A, e.g. vein.

AY – usually at the end of words, e.g. repay.

A–E – the most common long A spelling, e.g. stale.

AI – common in words ending in D, L, M, N, R, T.

O–E – the most common long O spelling, e.g. note.

OA – common in words ending in D, L, M, N, R, T.

OW – usually at the end of words, e.g. cow.

OU – usually at the start or in the middle of words, e.g. out, mouse.

Fifty words that are often misspelt

Learn them.

1. alcohol
2. although
3. autumn
4. beautiful
5. because
6. beginning
7. believe
8. business
9. chocolate
10. daughter
11. definitely
12. design
13. environment
14. February
15. forty
16. guard
17. happened
18. health
19. height
20. imaginary
21. interest
22. knowledge
23. listening
24. marriage
25. material
26. necessary
27. parallel
28. people
29. permanent
30. physical
31. possession
32. process
33. receive
34. remember
35. research
36. Saturday
37. secondary
38. separate
39. sincerely
40. soldier
41. stomach
42. straight
43. strength
44. success
45. surprise
46. technology
47. tomorrow
48. Wednesday
49. weight
50. women

Ten ways to remember spellings

- Break it into sounds (a-l-c-o-h-o-l).
- Break it into syllables (re-mem-ber).
- Break it into sections (re + search).
- Use a memory trick (necessary – one collar, two sleeves).
- Think of a word in the same family (e.g. strong – strength).
- Say it as it sounds (Wed-nes-day).
- Words within words (heal in health).
- Refer to etymology (Saturday = Saturn Day).
- Link to word families and learn a keyword (height, weight, freight, eight).
- Learning it by looking.

Soundalikes

These words are often mixed up. Here's a way to remember which is which:

Confusions	How to remember which is which
affect/effect	• *Affect* is what you do (verb) • *Effect* is the result (noun) • If you forget, use *effect* – it's used more often
allowed/aloud	• *Allowed* ends in ED because it's a past tense verb: *allow/allowed* • The word *loud* within *aloud* is a clue
bought/brought	• Say it slowly to hear the R • Link *brought* to *bring*
choose/chose	• OO says OO • Remember the double letter by remembering *Choose cheese*
cloth/clothe	• The E at the end makes the O long; compare *not/note*
our/are	• *Our* can be linked to the other pronoun *your*
practice/practise	• C is the noun • S is the verb • Easy-to-hear comparisons: *advice/advise* and *device/devise*
quiet/quite	• Say it slowly to hear the E before the T – it makes an extra syllable
threw/through	Learn: • I *knew* who *threw* it • *Through* the *rough* field
their/there	• Learn *their heirlooms* as a way of remembering which one means 'belonging to them' • Link *there* to *here* and *where*
to/too/two	• *To* is the most common one if you are not sure • The double O in *too* reminds you it means *too* many • *Two* links to *twice*

These are separate words:

• a lot of   • thank you

19. Notes to parents and helpers

This note contains advice about how to help a young person to compose a piece of writing, and then offers ideas for encouraging better writing.

Helping growing writers

Do you remember when they were very little, and you read a bedtime story? Or when they went to primary school how they brought home books and you listened to them read? The problem with writing is that no one ever writes a story at bedtime or listens to their children writing. It's not obvious how to share writing.

It's the same at school. There's plenty of help to get going, and there's marking afterwards, but something is missing in the middle – help at the time of writing.

This is how to do it.

Getting started

Sit with them before they start and get them to tell you what they have to do. Don't cross-question them: it makes them clam up.

Make sure they know these things before they start:

- the title or question
- the point of doing it
- how long it should be
- what style it should be.

And if you're lucky:

- what the teacher said about the task (if it is a school task)
- the mark scheme (sometimes pasted in the exercise book)
- if they're allowed to word process it.

Ask them to tell you the main things they need to say and what order to say them. This will be the writing plan. You write it. This is going to be harder than you think; it's surprising how often older children start writing without having a map of the writing in their heads. Ask clarifying questions as you go and finish by repeating back the order of points as you understand them.

If you or they find this really difficult, you may need to drop back to an earlier stage of gathering ideas.

Ask them how they're going to start. Some people find this incredibly challenging and they freeze up. If so, leave a space and you can go back to it later. Instead, start with the first proper point.

The process of writing

Ask them to tell you in their own words how they will express the first point or paragraph. If they seem pretty confident about it, get them to write it down and watch what they do.

Hold back on the criticism. It is really tempting to jump in at the first spelling error or offbeat expression and put it right. But don't do it. They will hate it and never want to write with you again. Also, don't do all the work for them even if it makes you feel good, because the idea is to help them to do it for themselves. On the other hand, approve of anything good such as:

- a well-chosen word
- a well-expressed idea
- a good opening line
- spelling a tricky word
- use of links, e.g. conversely, thus, although
- mature expression.

At the end of each paragraph, sum up what is good about the paragraph and allow yourself one other comment. Don't express it as a negative, and avoid interrogation. Make plain and obvious points and speak on your own behalf as a reader. For example:

- I think you've left a letter out of this word.
- I'm not clear what you're saying at the end here.
- So this is everything you want to say on this topic?
- This expression sounds odd to me.
- Check the punctuation in the middle there.
- I think you've missed a comma.

The idea is to alert them to the problem but let them sort it out. Don't abandon them, though. Allow a few moments for them to act. If they're plainly stuck, ask them to tell you what they're thinking.

- Tell me what you're thinking.
- What will you do?
- Tell me how you'll change it.
- Any ideas?

Now you can help by refining their ideas rather than substituting your own. Do this quickly. No slogging.

Getting on with it

Now let them get on with the writing for a while. It's too much to write the whole thing with them. Ask them to call you over when they get to a tricky bit.

The kitchen table is a pretty good place for writing because they can sit at it to write whilst you potter in the background. Stay around, avoid chatting and don't hover. And especially don't go sniping for errors.

When they're done, ask them to read the whole thing to you. This is for them more than it is for you. They will sense the effect of what they've written. Don't interrupt. Make at least two positive comments. Be specific – 'That's okay' won't do; you have to say what is okay, for example: 'The opening is strong, and you make a good point about newspapers.'

Depending on their mood, ask if they want you to proofread it for them or pick up on one point that was unclear during the reading.

Checking

If you proofread, indicate where the problems lie but don't correct them for them. Instead, give them a prompt:

- I think you've got a letter too many in that word – do you know which one it is?
- You've mixed up *there* and *their* – how do you know which is which?
- There's a full stop missing on this line – where should it go?
- There's a punctuation error on this line – can you see it?

Your main aim here is to teach them the right way to do it. But if they are struggling, don't slog. Tell them the general rule and how to correct the mistake. Let them correct it. Ideally, make a note that they can keep as an aide-mémoire. A sheet in a ring binder is good, or a sheet blu-tacked to the kitchen wall.

Showing an interest

You may find over the next day or so that the topic about which you were writing comes into your mind, or something will come up that reminds you of it. Mention it to your offspring: it's good that they know you found it interesting, that you looked beyond the spelling and punctuation. It says that writing has meaning.

Other things you can do to help

1. Help with written homework (but don't do it for them)

Make only constructive comments and ask questions such as these:

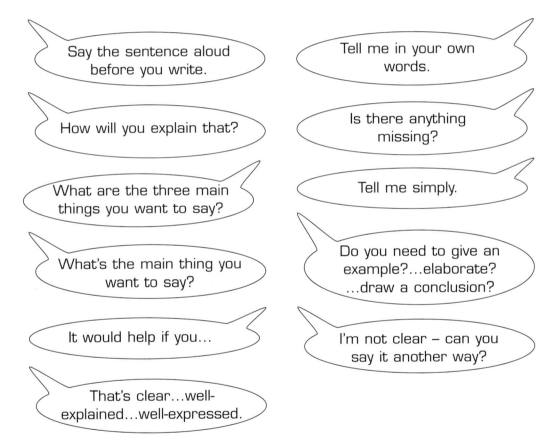

Say the sentence aloud before you write.

Tell me in your own words.

How will you explain that?

Is there anything missing?

What are the three main things you want to say?

Tell me simply.

What's the main thing you want to say?

Do you need to give an example?…elaborate? …draw a conclusion?

It would help if you…

I'm not clear – can you say it another way?

That's clear…well-explained…well-expressed.

2. Give gifts that encourage writing

e.g. diary, stationery, fountain pen, stamps, card-making software.

3. Play games that improve spelling

e.g. Scrabble, Boggle, Lexicon, crosswords, word searches.

4. Buy an easy-to-read dictionary and a thesaurus

Look for clear print, boldfaced words and simple explanations. Buy a respected brand.

5. Put up spelling checklists

Put them in places where they will be seen often, e.g. bedside, kitchen, bathroom mirror, toilet door.

6. Ask them to do writing for the family

e.g. shopping lists, packing lists, postcards, emails, thank you letters.

7. Encourage them to read more

Take them to visit libraries and bookshops. Read their set texts so you can discuss them. Point out interesting articles. Subscribe to a magazine. Buy book tokens. Introduce them to the Internet.

8. If they use a word processor, advise them how to use the facilities for checking, editing and presentation

The **checking** facilities include – the spellchecker, thesaurus, grammar check, word count and the track changes facilities. Most software has a setting that underlines spelling errors and grammatical issues as you type.

The **editing** facilities include cut, copy and paste.

The **presentation** facilities are usually listed under a drop-down format menu. It includes font size and shape, borders, shading, bullet styles, paragraph styles, etc. Many programmes now offer help with common layouts such as letters.

Some things that don't work

Forcing them to write

It's not really about writing more; it's about knowing how to compose. Practice is important at a certain stage, but you can end up recycling mistakes. If you want to write with your son or daughter, keep it to a few sentences and focus on expression.

Telling them what to write

If you tell them what to write, you'll get good at it but they will become dependent on you. The main thing is to help them do it for themselves. Ask helpful questions or make broad suggestions.

Expecting perfection

Stick to one or two points of help, and do it little and often. It's demoralising for them if you always expect perfection. Luckily, you have your children for life, so you can afford to take your time.

20. Notes to the teacher

Characteristics of writers at Level 3

The writers at whom this book is targeted are likely to be at Level 3 in writing, even if their reading is in advance of this. Already they will have a good grip on the simple sentence and be able to articulate ideas. Basic spellings and punctuation will be within their control. But undoubtedly, they will be feeling the pinch in secondary school because their sentences are too simple or too ill-controlled to carry the sophistication of meaning that is required by the curriculum. Their expression often lacks maturity, and sounds pedestrian or even naïve. Most Level 3 writers know enough to realise that their writing lacks something and it is a frustrating experience.

In terms of the National Curriculum, Level 3 writers are described thus:

> **Pupils' writing is often organised, imaginative and clear. The main features of different forms of writing are used appropriately, beginning to be adapted to different readers. Sequences of sentences extend ideas logically and words are chosen for variety and interest. The basic grammatical structure of sentences is usually correct. Spelling is usually accurate, including that of common, polysyllabic words. Punctuation to mark sentences – full stops, capital letters and question marks – is used accurately. Handwriting is joined and legible.**

But this is a 'best fit' descriptor: there will be many writers at Level 3 with wayward spelling, punctuation or expression and others who have absolute accuracy but without the inspiration to put it to good use. Notice the qualifying terms often, beginning to, and usually: the descriptor is at least realistic in recognising that the Level 3 writer has incomplete control.

In reality, there are two common types of writer at Level 3. The first can write an accurate sentence but not with flair. This writer is competent but unadventurous, accurate but limited. The other is an exciting but ill-disciplined writer who is frustrated that the flow of ideas will not gel into shapely sentences. This writer is expressive rather than elegant, and lacks articulation.

Moving from Level 3 to Level 4

Level 4 writers come across as much more confident and manipulative:

Pupils' writing in a range of forms is lively and thoughtful. Ideas are often sustained and developed in interesting ways and organised appropriately for the purpose of the reader. Vocabulary choices are often adventurous and words are used for effect. Pupils are beginning to use grammatically complex sentences, extending meaning. Spelling, including that of polysyllabic words that conform to regular patterns, is generally accurate. Full stops, capital letters and question marks are used correctly, and pupils are beginning to use punctuation within the sentence. Handwriting style is fluent, joined and legible.

Few teachers will argue with the ambitious vocabulary of this descriptor: *interesting, adventurous, complex, sustained, extended* – we all want that kind of writing. The problem lies in articulating these ambitious meanings into sentences that can carry them.

Success in writing is not about stamina or verbal wizardry; in fact, the best writing is often economic and plain. The descriptor is closer to the mark when it gestures towards *extended meaning, complex sentences* and *sustained meaning*. Pupils at Level 3 have to bring these under control if they are to progress.

The writer at Level 4 is trying to take control of language, beginning to test its potential to woo the reader and create effects. He or she is searching for a more sophisticated voice in writing, to carry the growing sense of self within him or her at this age. Sentences elongate, digress and qualify their meanings. Paragraphs and writing assignments are tailored to suit. New demands are placed on the writer who needs greater skill with punctuation to build more complex sentences, and spelling that must develop to contain a growing vocabulary.

What is so important about the complex sentence? Why does it confer exponential growth on pupils' powers of expression? The reason is that complex sentences yoke together different ideas to link, juxtapose, subordinate or qualify each other. The complex sentence empowers the writer because it can infer, shade and position meanings with precision, one against another; it can imply cause, significance, relationship; it offers subtlety and relationship and nuance. Command of the extended sentence is a quantum leap for a writer. It opens up new worlds of meaning.

In short, the pupil at Level 4 begins to use language as a plastic medium, bending and shaping it for his or her own ends. The defining feature of his or her work is a new consciousness of language as a tool and the beginnings of art. The writer is aware of composition.

The task of the teacher is to feed this growing capability with the skills and knowledge it needs to make meaning. Pupils moving towards Level 4 are pushing at the limits all the time, grappling with voice, structure and convention. They need advice and support. They need a teacher.

Using this book

This book is arranged in masterclasses to help the Level 4 writer to emerge. Each masterclass will fill two or maybe three lessons depending on the length of your lessons. The masterclasses break down quite easily so they can be spread in shorter blocks of around 20 minutes.

All the masterclasses are about the art of expression. Most of them are about sentences and a few are about paragraphs. Text level work is important, of course, but this book focuses on sentences because they have proved more difficult to teach in large classes.

The traditional way of teaching sentences at this level has been in the marking, but that comes too late. The important time is during composition itself, so this book attempts to address that shaping moment. The book is tightly structured to guide pupils through the process, leaving you free to work at close quarters with one or more pupils.

To add value, there are two things you can do:

- For key activities, demonstrate on the board how you would tackle them, composing on the spot and thinking aloud about what you are doing – why you choose particular words, why you delete particular words, what you are considering, what sounds wrong, what needs changing, what effect you're trying for and so on. The purpose of this is to give pupils an insight into the dynamics of composition.

- Take turns to sit by pupils who seem to struggle with writing and watch them compose. Ask them to talk aloud (as you have just done), to reveal to you the process they are going through. Your purpose is to unblock the process by giving them compositional strategies that work.

The masterclasses can be used flexibly but they could be arranged as:

- mini-units positioned between longer units of work
- group study units for up to six pupils
- guided writing groups
- a substantial unit of work on *Improving expression*.

Because you are expecting pupils to improve and revise their expression, they should be doing a lot of amendments. A word processor is an ideal tool, or failing this, a wipe-clean board for drafting. Paper gets very messy. To retain their amendments so that you can review their drafting, show them how to use the *Track Changes* facility which will record amendments but can also remove them at the touch of a button revealing the clean copy.

Also in this book are *Notes to parents and helpers* on page 110 and *Notes to the pupil* on page 100. As a minimum you should set these as reading homework. Even better, use them to set an agenda for a parents' evening on writing. As you work through the ideas and advice, get parents to try sample activities such as spotting words within words in a list of key spellings. Many schools offer evenings on reading, but writing evenings recruit just as well. If you have a video camera, they will be impressed to see a video showing a teacher working alongside a pupil. Sell them dictionaries, spelling games, writing materials and books. Parents and helpers are a valuable resource.

Acknowledgements

The author and publisher would like to thank the following for:

Copyright text:

p2 *St Agnes' Stand* © Thomas Eidson, 1994, Michael Joseph, by permission of PFD on behalf of Thomas Eidson; pp7, 8 and 15 *The Amber Spyglass* © Philip Pullman, 2000, the third and final volume of the *His Dark Materials* trilogy, published by Scholastic Children's Books. All rights reserved. Reproduced by permission of Scholastic Ltd; p8 *Journey through Britain* © John Hillaby, 1968, Constable & Co Ltd; pp13 and 14 *Fasting, Feasting* © Anita Desai, 1999, Chatto & Windus; pp16, 18, 20, 23 and 32 *The Midnight Fox* © Betsy Byars, 1968, Faber & Faber; pp17 and 18 *I am the Cheese* © Robert Cormier, 1977, Penguin; pp26, 27, 28, 29 and 30 *I'm the King of the Castle* © Susan Hill, 1970, Penguin; pp31 and 32 *Anita and Me* © Meera Syal, 1996, HarperCollins*Publishers*; p32 *The Lord of the Rings: The Two Towers* © J.R.R. Tolkien, 1954–55, HarperCollins*Publishers*; p34 *Sea Glass* © Anita Shreve, Time Warner Books UK; p40 *The Phantom Menace* © Patricia Wrede, 1999, Scholastic; p45 Emergency call information © British Telecommunications Plc; p51 *Hidden Depths* © Roger Hunt, 2002, Surrey Archaeological Society; pp56 and 59 *The BMA Complete Family Health Encyclopaedia* edited by Tony Smith © Dorling Kindersley, 1990; p67 *The Aimer Gate* © Alan Garner, 1978, Collins; pp70 and 71 *Abomination* © Robert Swindells, 1998, Doubleday; p73 *The Stream* © Brian Clarke, 2000, Swan Hill Press; p75 *The Watch House* © Robert Westall, 1977, Macmillan; pp77, 78 and 82 *The Sirius Crossing* © John Creed, 2002, Faber & Faber; p79 *The Chip-Chip Gatherers* © Shiva Naipaul, 1973, Deutsch; p80 *Bag and Baggage* © Judy Allen, 1988, Women's Press; p81 *Related Twilights* © Josef Herman, 1975, Robson Books; p83 *The Real Bravo Two Zero* © Michael Asher, 2002, Weidenfeld & Nicholson Military; p84 *Strange Boy* © Paul Magrs, 2002, Simon and Schuster; p92 'The Key' © John Gordon, from *The Burning Baby*, 1984, Walker Books; p94 *The Crocodile Hunter* © Steve and Terri Irwin, 2001, Dutton Books.

Copyright photos and images:

p3 *Leaking Tap* © Getty Stone images; p6 *Spider-Man* © The Ronald Grant Archive; p7 *Moonrise over Whitefish Lake* © Galen Rowell, CORBIS; p8 *Lightning*, Photodisk; p12 *Lance Armstrong* © actionplus sports images; p19 *Scaramouche* © The Ronald Grant Archive; p21 *Russian Dolls* © Emma Lee, Life File Photo Library; p23 *Red Fox in Black Phase* © Alissa Crandall, CORBIS; p24 *Traditional Feast* © Arthur Beck, CORBIS; p35 *Pebbles* © Angela Maynard, Life File Photo Library; p38 *Crying Shame* leaflet © Animal Aid; p40 *Mondays are Red* back cover © Hodder Children's Books; p40 *The Phantom Menace* © Lucasfilm, The Ronald Grant Archive; p42 *Running Out of Time* © Valerie Cambour, www.punishmentpark.com; p44 *Typetalk* © British Telecommunications Plc; p49 *Time Team* © Chris Bennett, Time Team, Videotext Communications Ltd in association with Picture House Television Co Ltd; p54 *Town Centre* © Jeremy Hoare, Life File Photo Library; p59 *Head Louse* © Andrew Syred, Science Photo Library; p83 *Michael Asher* © Owen Scurfield; p94 *Alligators* © Raymond Gehman, CORBIS; p98 *Girl Writing* © John Walmsley.

Copyright illustrations:

pp17 and 69 © Jo Blake, 2004, Beehive Illustration; p72 © Colin Brown, 2004, Beehive Illustration. All other artwork © Pete Smith, 2003, Beehive Illustration. Original artwork by Pete Smith coloured up by Richard Duszczak, Cartoon Studio Limited, 2004.

Every effort has been made to trace copyright holders of material reproduced in this book. Any rights not acknowledged here will be acknowledged in subsequent printings if notice is given to the publisher.